Samsung® Galaxy S® 4

FOR DUMMIES®

A Wiley Brand

Samsung® Galaxy S®4

FOR DUMMIES®

A Wiley Brand

by Bill Hughes

Samsung® Galaxy S® 4 For Dummies®

Published by
John Wiley & Sons, Inc.,
111 River Street,
Hoboken, NJ 07030-5774

www.wiley.com

Contents at a Glance

Table of Contents

Introduction

*T*he Samsung Galaxy S 4 is a powerful smartphone, perhaps the most powerful phone ever sold. As of the publication of this book, the Galaxy S 4 is the standard against which all other Android-based phones are measured.

Each cellular carrier offers a slightly customized version of the Galaxy S 4. Some cellular carriers' phones come out of the box with preloaded applications, games, or files. Some come with accessories, like a corded headset, whereas others don't. This book doesn't dwell on these kinds of differences.

Although the name for each network is different, these phones are largely the same (at least one marketing person at each cellular carrier is cringing as you read this). This allows me to write this book in a way that covers the common capabilities.

At a core level, these phones are built for high-speed wireless communications. The cellular carriers have spent kajillions upgrading their networks to offer more coverage and better data speeds than their competition. Again, this book doesn't dwell on these differences in network technology because they don't really make much difference (again, at least one engineering person at each cellular carrier is cringing as you read this).

I assume that you already have a phone, and I just hope that you have good coverage where you spend more of your time with your phone. If so, you will be fine. If not, you need to switch to another network because the experience with your phone will be frustrating. I would advise you to return your phone to that carrier and buy another Galaxy S 4 at another cellular carrier. As long as you have good cellular data coverage, owning a Galaxy S 4 will be an exciting experience!

First, all Galaxy S phones use Google's Android platform. This is the equivalent of different brands of PCs all being based upon Microsoft's Windows operating system. Although there are some differences in how the operating system appears when you turn on your PC for the first time, the experience is largely similar whether the PC comes from Dell or from HP. (Now at least two PC product managers, one at Dell and the other at HP, are cringing.) This is in contrast to the experience you have when you bring up a PC running Ubuntu Linux, which is noticeably different.

The good news is that the Android platform has proven to be widely popular, even more successful than Google originally expected when it first announced it in November of 2007. More people are using Android-based phones, and more third parties are writing applications. This is good news because it offers you more options for applications (more on this in Chapter 8 on the Play Store, where you buy applications).

In addition, all Galaxy S 4 phones use a powerful graphics processor, employ Samsung's super-bright AMOLED touchscreen, and are covered in Corning's Gorilla Glass. The superior screen experience differentiates this product line from other Android phones. Because of these enhanced capabilities, you can navigate around the screen with multi-touch screens instead of hierarchical menus that are found on lesser Android phones. Plus, the videos look stunning from many angles.

Smartphones are getting smarter all the time, and the Galaxy S 4 is one of the smartest. However, just because you've used a smartphone in the past doesn't mean you should expect to use your new Galaxy S 4 without a bit of guidance.

You may not be familiar with using a multi-touch screen, and your new phone offers a lot of capabilities that you may or may not be familiar with. It would be unfortunate to find out from a kid in the neighborhood that the phone you have been carrying around for several months could solve a problem you have been having because you were never told that the solution was in your pocket the whole time.

In fact, Samsung is proud of the usability of its entire Galaxy S lineup. It is so proud that the user's manual is really just a "quickstart" guide. You can find instructions on the web. However, you have to know what you don't know to get what you want unless you plan to view every tutorial.

That's where this book comes in. This book is a hands-on guide to getting the most out of your Galaxy S 4.

About This Book

This book is a reference — you don't have to read it from beginning to end to get all you need out of it. The information is clearly organized and easy to access. You don't need thick glasses to understand this book. This book helps you figure out what you want to do — and then tells you how to do it in plain English.

I don't use many conventions in this book, but here are a few you should know about:

- Whenever I introduce a new term, I put it in *italics* and define it shortly thereafter (often in parentheses).
- I use **bold** for the action parts of numbered steps, so you can easily see what you're supposed to do.

✔ I use `monofont` for web addresses and e-mail addresses, so they stand out from the surrounding text. If you're reading this as an e-book, these links are live and clickable. ***Note:*** When this book was printed, some web addresses may have needed to break across two lines of text. If that happened, rest assured that we haven't put in any extra characters (such as hyphens) to indicate the break. So, when using one of these web addresses, just type in exactly what you see in this book, pretending as though the line break doesn't exist.

What You're Not to Read

I think you'll find every last word of this book scintillating, but I may be a little biased. The truth is, you don't have to read

✔ **Sidebars:** Sidebars are those gray boxes throughout the book. They're interesting, but not essential to the topic at hand, so if you're short on time or you want only the information you absolutely need, you can skip them.

✔ **Text marked with the Technical Stuff icon:** For more on this icon, see the "Icons Used in This Book" section, later in this Introduction.

Foolish Assumptions

You know what they say about assuming, so I don't do much of it in this book. But I do make a few assumptions about you:

✔ **You have a Galaxy S 4 phone.** You may be thinking about buying a Galaxy S 4 phone, but my money's on your already owning one. After all, getting your hands on the phone is the best part!

✔ **You're not totally new to cellphones.** You know that your Galaxy S 4 phone is capable of doing more than the average cellphone, and you're eager to find out what your phone can do.

✔ **You've used a computer.** You don't have to be a computer expert, but you at least know how to check your e-mail and surf the web.

How This Book Is Organized

The 18 chapters in this book are divided into six parts. Here's what you can find in each part.

Part I: Getting Started with the Samsung Galaxy S 4

The first part of this book gets you familiar with the basic capabilities of your Galaxy S 4 phone. Chapters 1 and 2 are an introduction to everything from turning it on and off, to understanding cellular billing, to managing battery life.

Part II: Communications

In this part, I walk you through the basic capabilities of the Galaxy S 4 for communicating with voice, texts, and e-mails. Chapter 3 is about making calls. Chapter 4 covers what you need to know about texting. Chapter 5 covers e-mailing, and Chapter 6 explores how the phone works with your Contacts database.

Part III: Live on the Internet: Going Mobile

This part is all about the Internet — how to access it from your Galaxy S 4 phone. I also introduce you to the Play Store, where you can trick out your phone with more apps.

Part IV: Entertainment Applications

An important use for many smartphone owners involves entertainment. Chapter 9 covers the impressive picture-taking capabilities of your phone but really covers only some of the capabilities. Chapter 10 looks at the impressive gaming capabilities, whereas Chapter 11 explores navigating to all the fun places you can go in the real world. Chapter 12 walks you through playing music and video on your phone.

Part V: Productivity Applications

In this part, I cover the capabilities of the Galaxy S 4 smartphone that make you more productive at home and work.

Part VI: The Part of Tens

This wouldn't be a *For Dummies* book without a Part of Tens. In this book, the Part of Tens covers ten ways to customize the phone to make it truly your own, how to keep your information safe, and ten capabilities to look for in future releases.

Icons Used in This Book

Throughout this book, I used *icons* (little pictures in the margin) to draw your attention to various types of information. Here's a key to what those icons mean:

This whole book is like one series of tips. When I share especially useful tips and tricks, I mark it with the Tip icon.

This book is a reference, which means you don't have to commit it to memory — there is no test at the end. But once in a while, I do tell you things that are so important that I think you should remember them, and when I do, I mark them with the Remember icon.

Whenever you may do something that could cause a major headache, I warn you with the, er, Warning icon.

When you see this icon, you'll find interesting but optional information you can skip if you like.

Beyond the Book

This book has more great online extras. To access the book's online cheat sheet, go to www.dummies.com/cheatsheet/samsunggalaxys4. To read articles about the Samsung Galaxy S 4, go to www.dummies.com/extras/ samsunggalaxys4.

Occasionally, we have updates to our technology books. If this book does have technical updates, they will be posted at dummies.com/go/samsung galaxys4fdupdates.

Where to Go from Here

You don't have to read this book from cover to cover. You can skip around as you like. For example, if you need the basics on calling, texting, and e-mailing, turn to Part II. To discover more about photos, games, and apps, go to Part IV. To find out about the phone's calendar functions or S-Voice, turn to Part V.

Part I

Getting Started with the Samsung Galaxy S 4

 Visit www.dummies.com/extras/samsunggalaxys4 for great Dummies content online.

In this part . . .

- ✔ Reviewing the basic capabilities of just about any cellphone and what sets smartphones apart

- ✔ Navigating your phone for the first time

- ✔ Turning off your phone and managing sleep mode

Exploring What You Can Do with Your Phone

In This Chapter

▶ Reviewing the basic capabilities of just about any cellphone

▶ Understanding what sets smartphones apart

▶ Mapping out what makes Samsung Galaxy S 4 phones so cool

*W*hether you want just the basics from a phone (make and take phone calls, customize your ringtone, take some pictures, maybe use a Bluetooth headset) or you want your phone to be always by your side (a tool for multiple uses throughout your day), you can make that happen. In this chapter, I outline all the things your phone can do — from the basics, to what makes Galaxy S 4 phones different from the rest. Throughout the remainder of the book, I walk you through the steps you need to take to get your phone doing what makes you the happiest.

Discovering the Basics of Your Phone

All cellphones on the market today include basic functions, and even some entry-level phones are a little more sophisticated. Of course, Samsung includes all basic functions on the Galaxy S 4 model. In addition to making and taking calls (see Chapter 3) and sending and receiving texts (see Chapter 4), the Galaxy S 4 sports the following basic features:

- **13MP digital camera:** This resolution is more than enough for posting good-quality images on the Internet and even having 4" x 6" prints made.

- **Ringtones:** You can replace the standard ringtone with custom ringtones that you download to your phone. You also can specify different rings for different numbers.

- **Bluetooth:** The Galaxy S 4 phone supports stereo and standard Bluetooth devices. (See Chapter 3 for more on Bluetooth.)

- **High-resolution screen:** The Galaxy S 4 phone offers one of the highest-resolution touchscreens on the market (1920×1080 pixels).

- **Capacitive touchscreen:** The Galaxy S 4 phone offers a very slick touchscreen that's sensitive enough to allow you to interact with the screen accurately but not so sensitive that it's hard to manage. In addition, it has an optional setting that steps up the sensitivity in case you need to use your phone while wearing gloves.

Taking Your Phone to the Next Level: The Smartphone Features

In addition to the basic capabilities of any entry-level cellphone, the Galaxy S 4 phone, which is based upon the popular Android platform, has capabilities associated with other smartphones, such as the Apple iPhone and the phones based upon Windows Phone 8:

- **Internet access:** Access websites through a web browser on your phone.

- **Photos:** The phone comes with a camera but also the ability to manage photos.

- **Wireless e-mail:** Send and receive e-mail from your phone.

- **Multimedia:** Play music and videos on your phone.

- **Contact Manager:** The Galaxy S 4 phone lets you take shortcuts from having to enter someone's ten-digit number each time you want to call or text them. In fact, the Contact Manager has the ability to track all the numbers that an individual might have plus their e-mail address and photo. On top of that, it can synchronize with the contact manager on both your personal and work PCs!

- **Digital camcorder:** The Galaxy S 4 phone comes with a built-in digital camcorder that records at a resolution that you can set, including HD.

- **Mapping and directions:** The Galaxy S 4 phone uses the GPS (Global Positioning System) in your phone to tell you where you are, find local services that you need, and give you directions to where you want to go.

- **Business applications:** The Galaxy S 4 can keep you productive while you're away from the office.

I go into each of these capabilities in greater detail in the following sections.

Internet access

Until a few years ago, the only way to access the Internet when you were away from a desk was with a laptop. Smartphones are a great alternative to laptops because they're small, convenient, and ready to launch their web browsers right away. Even more important, when you have a smartphone, you can access the Internet wherever you are — whether Wi-Fi is available or not.

The drawback to smartphones, however, is that their screen size is less than even the most basic laptop screen. The pixel resolution is there, but the raw real estate of the screen is not. Plus, image-heavy websites can take a long time to load. To accommodate this problem, more websites are adding mobile versions. These sites are slimmed-down versions of their main site with fewer images but similar access to the information on the site. These site names usually begins with `m` or `mobile`, such as `m.yahoo.com`.

Figure 1-1 shows the regular website for Refdesk.com on the left and its mobilized version on the right. The mobilized version has no pictures and is more vertically oriented.

Figure 1-1: A mobile website is a slimmed-down version of the main site.

On the Galaxy S 4 phone, you can use the mobile version of a website if you want, but if you prefer to use the standard website, you can pinch and stretch your way to get the information you want — see Chapter 2 for more information on pinching and stretching.

For more information on accessing the Internet from your Galaxy S 4 phone, turn to Chapter 7.

Photos

The image application on your phone helps you use the digital camera on your Galaxy S 4 phone to its full potential. Studies have found that cellphone users tend to snap a bunch of pictures within the first month of phone usage. After that, the photos sit on the phone (instead of being downloaded to a computer), and the picture-taking rate drops dramatically.

The Galaxy S 4 phone image management application is different. You can integrate your camera images into your home photo library, as well as photo-sharing sites such as Picasa and Flickr, with minimal effort.

For more on how to use the Photo applications, you can turn to Chapter 9.

Wireless e-mail

On your Galaxy smartphone, you can access your business and personal e-mail accounts, reading and sending e-mail messages on the go. Depending on your e-mail system, you might be able to sync so that when you delete an e-mail on your phone, the e-mail is deleted on your computer at the same time so you don't have to read the same messages on your phone and your computer.

Chapter 6 covers setting up your business and personal e-mail accounts.

Multimedia

Some smartphones allow you to play music and videos on your phone in place of a dedicated MP3 or video player. On the Galaxy S 4 phone, you can use the applications that come with the phone, or you can download applications that offer these capabilities from the Play Store.

Chapter 12 covers how to use the multimedia services with your Galaxy S 4 phone.

Business applications

Whether your company gives you a Galaxy S 4 phone for work or you buy your Galaxy S 4 phone yourself, the Galaxy S 4 phone offers you the ability to work on Microsoft Office applications.

Chapter 14 explores how to set up your phone to work with Microsoft Office applications.

Customizing Your Phone with Games and Applications

Application developers — large and small — are working on the Android platform to offer a variety of applications and games for the Galaxy S 4 phone. Compared to most of the other smartphone platforms, Google imposes on application developers fewer restrictions on what is allowable. This freedom to develop resonates with many developers, resulting in a bonanza of application development on this platform.

As of this writing, more than 700,000 applications are available from Google's Play Store. For more information about downloading games and applications, turn to Chapter 8.

Downloading games

Chapter 10 of this book is for gamers. Although your phone comes with a few general-interest games, you can find a whole wide world of games for every skill and taste. In Chapter 10, I give you all the information you need to set up different gaming experiences. Whether you prefer standalone games or multiplayer games, you can set up your Galaxy S 4 phone to get what you need.

Downloading applications

Your phone comes with some very nice applications, but these might not take you as far as you want to go. You might also have some special interests, like philately or stargazing, that neither Samsung nor your carrier felt would be of sufficient general interest to include on the phone. (Can you imagine?)

You phone also comes with preloaded *widgets,* which are smaller applications that serve a particular purpose, such as retrieving stock quotes or telling you how your phone's battery is feeling today. They reside on the extended Home Screen and are instantly available.

Buying applications allows you to get additional capabilities quickly, easily, and inexpensively. Ultimately, these make your phone, which is already a reflection of who you are, more personal as you add more capabilities.

Take a deep breath

You don't have to rush to implement every feature of your Galaxy S 4 phone the very first day you get it. Instead, pick one capability at a time. Digest it, enjoy it, and then tackle the next one.

I recommend starting with setting up your e-mail and social accounts, but that's just me.

No matter how you tackle the process of setting up your Galaxy S 4 phone, it'll take some time. If you try to cram it all in on the first day, you'll turn what should be fun into drudgery.

The good news is that you own the book that takes you through the process. You can do a chapter or two at a time.

What's cool about the Android platform

The Samsung Galaxy S 4 phone is the top-of-the-line Android phone. That means that any application developed for an Android phone will run to its full capability. This is significant because one of the founding principles in the creation of the Android platform is to create an environment where application developers can be as creative as possible without an oppressive organization dictating what can and cannot be sold (as long as it's within the law, of course). This has inspired many of the best applications developers to go with Android first.

On top of that, Android is designed to run multiple applications at once. Other smartphone platforms have added this capability, but Android is designed for you to be able to jump quickly among multiple apps that you're running — and that makes your experience that much smoother.

You and Your Shadow: Understanding How Your Cellular Carrier Bills You

In the United States, most cellular companies sell phones at a significant discount when you sign up for a service agreement. And most cellular companies offer discounts on phones when you want to upgrade to something newer (as long as you also sign up for another couple of years of service). So, it's not surprising that most people buy their phones directly from cellular companies.

If your new Galaxy S 4 phone device is an upgrade from an older phone, you might have a service plan that was suitable with your last phone but isn't so great anymore. If this is your first cellphone (ever, or with this particular carrier), you might start with an entry-level plan, thinking you wouldn't need "that many minutes," only to find that you and your phone are inseparable, and you need a better plan. The good news is that most cellular carriers allow you to change your service plan.

Most cellular service plans have three components of usage:

- Voice
- Text
- Data

I walk you through each of these components and how they affect using your Galaxy S 4 in the following sections.

Voice usage

Voice usage is the most common, costly, and complex element of most service plans. Cellular providers typically offer plans with a certain number of anytime minutes and a certain number of night/weekend minutes. Some providers offer plans with reduced rates (or even free calls) to frequently called numbers, to other cellphones with the same cellular provider, or to other cellphones in general. If you talk a lot, you might be able to opt for an unlimited voice plan (for domestic calls only).

At its core, a Galaxy S 4 phone device is, obviously, a phone. In the early days of smartphones, manufacturers were stung by the criticism that smartphones weren't as easy to use as traditional cellphones. Indeed, you do have to bring up the phone screen to make a call (more on making and receiving calls in Chapter 3). As an improvement, Samsung has made sure that the screen used to make calls is only one click away from the Home screen.

 If keeping track of minutes is important to you and your calling plan, be mindful of all those e-mails and social network updates that prompt you to call someone right away. You might be tempted to make more calls than you did with your old (dumb) cellular phone.

Text usage

A texting "bundle" is an add-on to your voice plan. Some service plans include unlimited texting; others offer a certain number of text messages for a flat rate. For example, maybe you pay an additional $5 per month to get 200 free text messages — meaning that combined, you can send and receive a *total* of 200 messages per month. If you go over that limit, you pay a certain amount per message (usually more for text messages you send than those you receive).

As with voice, the Galaxy S 4 phone makes it very convenient to text, making it more likely that you'll use this service and end up using more texts than you expect. However, nothing obligates you to buy a texting plan.

My advice is to get at least some texting capability but be ready to decide if you want to pay for more or stay with a minimal plan and budget your texts.

What if I didn't get my phone from a cellular company?

With a few exceptions, such as an "unlocked" GSM phone, each phone is associated with a particular cellular company. (In this context, a *locked* phone can work only on its original carrier.) Maybe you bought a secondhand phone on eBay, or you got a phone from a friend who didn't want his anymore. If you didn't get your phone directly from a cellular provider, you will need to figure out which provider the phone is associated with and get a service plan from that company. Some Galaxy S 4 phones sold in the United States all have the cellular company's logo on the phone printed on the front. That makes it easy to know which carrier a phone will operate with.

If there is not a logo on the front, you need to figure out which cellular carrier it can work with. The quickest way is to take the phone to any cellular store; the folks there know how to figure it out.

To narrow down the possibilities on your own, you need to do some investigation. The easiest way is to take off the back of the phone to find the plate with the model and serial number for the phone. If you see IMEI on the plate, the phone is based on a technology called Global System for Mobile (GSM); it'll work with AT&T or T-Mobile (or both). If you see ESN on the plate, the phone will work with either Verizon or Sprint (but not both).

Data usage

Although getting texting may be optional, access to the Internet is essential to get the full experience of your Galaxy S 4 phone. The Internet is where you access the capabilities that make the Galaxy S 4 phone so special. Some cellular carriers may let you use the phone on their network without a data plan. I cannot imagine why you would want to do that. Although your phone will supplement the coverage you get from your cellular carrier with Wi-Fi, you really need to have a data plan from your cellular carrier to get most of the value out of your investment in your phone. There's just no getting around it.

Most cellular companies price Internet access with usage increments measured in the hundreds of megabytes (MB) but more often in gigabytes (GB).

As of this writing, Sprint makes it easy by only offering unlimited data. This is good news: As you customize your phone to keep up with your friends and access your favorite sites, the cost of access won't increase.

Other carriers offer an unlimited option but at a higher price. It is a challenge to figure out how much data you are going to need without going over the limit and paying a usage penalty. Some carriers try to help you by giving you some tools to estimate your usage by estimating the number of e-mails, web pages, or multimedia files you plan to download.

These are iffy. One option is to go with the lowest increment of data, unless you plan to be downloading a large number of videos, but using some of the tools I cover later to see how much data you are actually using.

Another school of thought is to go for an increment of data larger than you think you'll need. After you have some experience with how much data you actually use, you can call your carrier to scale back your usage if appropriate.

Don't blame me if you do not check your usage! It's easy to check and increase your usage, even mid-billing cycle.

Another consideration: Family plans

A popular option is to combine your usage of voice, text, and data with your family members. The family unit on the plan gets to share a fixed allotment of voice minutes, texts, and data. This works well, as long as a responsible person checks your usage during the billing period!

Yet one more consideration: International usage

If you travel internationally with your Galaxy S 4, you should check with your carrier about your billing options before you travel. Voice and text are usually not too bad when you roam internationally. Data is another story.

Rates for data when roaming internationally can be very high. You can end up with a very unpleasant situation if you do not check and plan accordingly.

One final consideration: Web subscription fees

Don't forget that some web-based services charge subscription fees. For example, WeatherBug offers a consumer service that gives you weather conditions, but it also offers WeatherBug Pro that provides more information — with a monthly fee to subscribers. Yup, if you want WeatherBug Pro on your phone, you have to pay the piper. Some of these services can be billed through your cellular carrier (check first), but just make sure you're willing to pony up for the service.

Surviving Unboxing Day

When you turn on your phone the first time, it will ask you a series of ten questions and preferences to configure it. Frankly, they are trying to make this book unnecessary and put me out of business. The nerve!

The good folks at Samsung are well intentioned, but not every one of their customers of the Samsung Galaxy S 4 knows from day one whether she wants a Samsung account, what's a good name for her phone, or what the purpose of a drop box is, much less whether she wants to bother to sign up for one.

You can relax. I'll help you answer these questions, or, when appropriate, I refer you to the chapter within this book that helps you come up with your answer.

On the other hand, if your phone is already set up, you probably took a guess or skipped some questions. Maybe now you're rethinking some of your choices. No problem. You can go back and change any answer you gave and get your phone to behave the way you want.

The questions are as follows:

- ✔ **Screen 1: Language/Accessibility:** This option lets you select your language. The default is English for phones sold within the United States. Also, the phone has some special capabilities for individuals with disabilities. If you have a disability and think you might benefit, take a look at these options.

- ✔ **Screen 2: Wi-Fi:** Your phone automatically starts scanning for a Wi-Fi connection. You can always use the cellular connection when you are in cellular coverage, but if there is a Wi-Fi connection available, your phone will try to use this first. It is probably cheaper and may be faster than the cellular.

  At the same time, you may not want your phone to connect to the Wi-Fi access point with the best signal. It could be that the strongest signal is a fee-based service, whereas the next best signal is free. In any case, this page scans the available options and presents them to you. If you need to enter a password, you'll see the screen in Figure 1-2.

Figure 1-2: The pop-up window for a Wi-Fi password.

If this is all too much to take in right now, feel free to skip to the next screen.

✔ **Screen 3: Date and Time:** This is easy. The default setting is to use the time and date that comes from the cellular network. Just tap on the next button and move on. This date and time from the cellular network is the most accurate information you will get, and you do not need to do anything other than be within cellular coverage now and again.

✔ **Screen 4: Sign up for a Samsung Account:** My advice is to skip this screen for now. The Samsung account offers you some nice things such as backing up your phone information and access to music, movies, and video. At the same time, there is so much more out there that it is best to forge ahead and leave this for another time.

✔ **Screen 5: Google Account Sign-up:** "Google account" means an e-mail account where the address ends in @gmail.com. If you already have an account on Gmail, enter your user ID and password here. If you do not have a Gmail account, I suggest waiting until you read Chapter 5. I recommend that you create a Gmail account, but it is best to go through some other steps first.

✔ **Screen 6: Location Options:** Your phone knowing your location and providing it to an application can be a sensitive issue.

If you are really worried about privacy and security, tap the green checkmarks on the screen and then tap the button that says Next. Selecting these options prevents applications from knowing where you are. This prevents you from getting directions and a large number of cool capabilities that are built into applications. The only folks who will know your location are the 911 dispatchers if you dial them.

If you are worried about your security but may want to take advantage of some of the cool capabilities built into your phone, tap the right arrow key to move forward. Remember, you can choose on a case-by-case basis whether to share your location. I cover this more in Chapter 8.

✔ **Screen 7: Phone Ownership:** This screen asks you to enter your first and last name. You may ask why this is important at this point. It's not. If you have been able to navigate this far, you may be ready to tap in your first and last name. If not, just tap the right arrow. All will be fine.

✔ **Screen 9: Dropbox:** This is a generous offer, but what is it for? I explain this more in Chapter 14. You may or may not ever need this. If you do, you can come back and take them up on this later. For now, just tap Skip.

✔ **Screen 10: Learn about key features:** If you think you don't need this book, go ahead and take this tour of all the new things you can do. If you think you might need this book in any way, shape, or form, tap the Next button. This screen is for setting up the coolest and the most-sophisticated capabilities of the phone. I cover many of them in the course of this book. For now, skip this to get to the last screen.

✔ **Screen 11: Device Name:** When this screen comes up, you'll see a text box that has the model name. You can keep this name or you can choose to personalize it a bit. For example, you can change it to "Bill's Galaxy S 4" or "Indy at 425-555-1234." The purpose of this name is for connecting to a local data network, such as when you are pairing to a Bluetooth device. If this last sentence made no sense to you, don't worry about it. Tap Finish. In a moment, you see the Home screen, as shown in Figure 1-3.

Figure 1-3: The Home screen for the Samsung Galaxy S 4.

Beginning at the Beginning

*I*n this chapter, I fill you in on the basics of using your new Samsung Galaxy S 4. You start by turning on your phone. (I told you I was covering the basics!) I guide you through charging your phone and getting the most out of your phone's battery. Stick with me for a basic tour of your phone's buttons and other features. Then I end by telling you how to turn off your phone or put it in "sleep" mode.

Unless you're new to cellphones in general — and smartphones in particular — you might want to skip this chapter. If the term "smartphone" is foreign to you, you probably haven't used one before, and reading this chapter won't hurt. And, just so you know, a *smartphone* is just a cellular phone on which you can download and run applications that are better than what comes preloaded on a phone right out of the box.

First Things First: Turning On Your Phone

When you open the box of your new phone, the packaging will present you with your phone, wrapped in plastic, readily accessible. If you haven't already, take the phone out of the plastic bag and remove any protective covering material on the screen.

First things first. The On button is on the right side of the phone. You can see the symbol on the button in Figure 2-1. Press the On button for a second, and see whether it vibrates and the screen lights up. Hopefully, your phone arrived with enough electrical charge that you won't have to plug it in to an outlet right away. You can enjoy your new phone for the first day without having to charge it.

The On button

Figure 2-1: The On button on the phone.

The phones that you get at the stores of most cellular carriers usually come with the battery installed, partially charged, and registered with the network.

If the screen does light up, don't hold the On button too long, or the phone might turn off.

If the phone screen doesn't light up (rats), you need to charge the battery. Here's the rub: It's important to fully charge the battery for 24 hours, or at least overnight, so that it will last as long as possible. That means that you have wait to use your beautiful new phone. Sorry.

Of course, it's possible that the battery needs to be inserted in the first place. To do this, you need to open the case. This isn't the end of the world, though. In fact, you should learn to do this sooner or later, anyway, so keep reading to see how.

The peel-off back for the Galaxy S 4

To expose the slots for the optional memory card, SIM card, and the battery slot, you remove the back by slipping a fingernail under the back cover. There is a small slot to make this easier on the right side towards the top of the phone; see its location in Figure 2-2.

Don't use a sharp object, like a knife, to peel off the back of the phone. You might get away with that once or twice, but you'll end up scratching the plastic. If you have chewed your nails to the nubbins, ask someone with fingernails to do it for you — or use something plastic, like a credit card.

If you look at the bottom of the phone, there is something that looks like a nice, large slot that you can use to peel off the back of the phone. This is actually a micro-USB port where you connect your phone to be charged. Don't try to remove the back of the phone by using this port. If you stick a knife or something sharp in this port, you will probably damage the micro-USB port and no longer be able to charge your phone!

Open the cover here.

Figure 2-2: Open the cover from the slot at the top of your phone.

Now that you have the back off . . .

Without the back, you can see the insides of your phone, as shown in Figure 2-3.

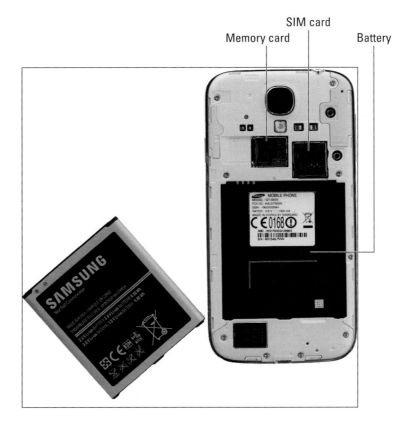

SIM card

Memory card   Battery

Figure 2-3: The insides of your phone.

From here, you can insert or remove the following components, as needed:

- ✔ The battery (you can't miss it).
- ✔ The MicroSD card to store files, music, and video (more on this in Chapters 9 and 12).
- ✔ Your SIM card. (More on SIM cards in Chapter 6.)

In each case, look for a small engraving or printed image that shows you the correct orientation for the MicroSD card and the SIM card. It might be small and faint, but it's there!

Putting in and taking out the MicroSD card (Figure 2-4) is easy. You may want to practice, but be careful not to lose it. It is about the size of the fingernail on your little finger.

Figure 2-4: The MicroSD card.

To remove a MicroSD card from the port, push it in just a bit with your fingernail, and it will spring out like toast out of a toaster.

If you try to force the micro SD card out simply by pulling it out, you will ruin the card.

You may have noticed that it is important to have fingernails with the Samsung Galaxy S 4. If you ever recommend the Galaxy S 4 to a friend, you may also want to suggest that she get a manicure beforehand.

Charging Your Phone and Managing Battery Life

Although you probably don't have to plug your phone into an outlet right away, the first time you do plug it in, allow it to charge overnight.

TECHNICAL STUFF

The nitty-gritty of how your phone works

As soon as you turn on your phone, several things happen. As the phone is powering up, it begins transmitting information to and receiving information from nearby cellular towers. The first information exchanged includes your phone's electronic serial number. Every cellphone has its own unique serial number built into the hardware of the phone; the serial number in current-generation cellphones can't be duplicated or used by any other phone.

The technical name of this electronic serial number depends on your cellular carrier. AT&T, T-Mobile, and U.S. Cellular call it an International Mobile Equipment Identity (IMEI) number. Verizon and Sprint refer to it as an electronic serial number (ESN).

It doesn't matter to the phone or the cellular tower if you're near your home when you turn on your phone — and that's the joy of cellphones. All cellular networks have agreements that allow you to use cellular networks in other parts of the country and, sometimes, around the world.

That said, a call outside your cellular provider's own network may be expensive. Within the United States, many service plans allow you to pay the same rate if you use your phone anywhere in the United States to call anywhere in the United States. If you travel outside the United States, even to Canada, you might end up paying through the nose. Remember: Before you leave on a trip, check with your cellular carrier about your rates. Even if you travel internationally only a few times yearly, a different service plan may work better for you. Your cellular carrier can fill you in on your options.

You'll hear all kinds of "battery lore" left over from earlier battery technologies. For example, lithium-ion (Li-ion) batteries don't have a "memory" like nickel-cadmium (NiCad) batteries did. And the Samsung Galaxy S 4 does use Li-ion batteries. That means that you don't have to be careful to allow the battery to fully discharge before recharging it.

Your phone comes with a two-piece battery charger (cable and the transformer), as shown in Figure 2-5.

The cable has two ends: one end that plugs into the phone, and the other that's a standard USB connector. The phone end is a small connector called a micro USB that is used on some Samsung devices and is becoming the standard for charging cell phones and other small electronics, and for connecting them to computers.

Figure 2-5: The transformer and USB cable for charging your phone.

To charge the phone, you have two choices:

- ✔ Plug the transformer into a wall socket and then plug the cable's USB plug into the USB receptacle in the transformer.
- ✔ Plug the USB on the cable into a USB port on your PC.

Then you plug the small end of the cable into the phone. The port is on the bottom of the phone. Make sure you push the little metal plug all the way in.

It doesn't really matter in what order you plug in things. However, if you use the USB port on a PC, the PC needs to be powered on for the phone to charge.

Unplug the transformer when you aren't charging your phone. A charger left plugged in will draw a small but continuous stream of power.

If your phone is Off when you're charging the battery, an image of a battery displays onscreen for a moment. The green portion of the battery indicates the amount of charge within the battery. You can get the image to reappear with a quick press of the Power button. This gives you the status of the battery without your having to turn on the phone.

If your phone is On, you see a small battery icon at the top of the screen showing how much charge is in the phone's battery. When the battery in the phone is fully charged, it vibrates to let you know that it's done and that you should unplug the phone and charger.

It takes only a few hours to go from a dead battery to a fully charged battery. Other than the first time you charge the phone, you don't need to wait for the battery to be fully charged. You can partially recharge and run if you want.

In addition to the transformer and USB cable that comes with the phone, you have other optional charging tools:

- **Travel USB charger:** If you already have a USB travel charger, you can leave the transformer at home. This will run you about $15. You still need your cable, although any USB-to-micro USB cable should work.

- **Car charger:** You can buy a charger with a USB port that plugs into the power socket/cigarette lighter in a car. This is convenient if you spend a lot of time in your car. The list price is $30, but you can get the real Samsung car charger for less at some online stores.

- **Photocell or fuel cell charger:** Several companies make products that can charge your phone. Some use photovoltaic cells to transform light into power. As long as there is a USB port (the female part of the USB), all you need is your cable. These can cost from $40 to $100 on up.

Ideally, use Samsung chargers. And if you don't, make sure that any options you use from the preceding list are from a reputable manufacturer. The power specifications for USB ports are standardized. Reputable manufactures comply with these standards, but less reputable manufacturers might not. Cheap USB chargers physically fit the USB end of the cable that goes to your phone. However, Li-ion batteries are sensitive to voltage, and an off-brand USB charger can hurt the performance of your battery.

Li-ion batteries do not like extreme heat. A warm room is one thing, but if you leave your phone on the dashboard all day in Phoenix during the summer, your battery will die. If your phone is with you and you can stand the heat, your battery will be fine.

If you take good care of it, your battery should last about two years, with a drop in performance of about 25 percent from pristine condition out of the box. At that point, you can replace the battery or upgrade to the newest Galaxy S phone.

Navigating the Galaxy S 4

Galaxy S 4 phone devices differ from other phones in that they have significantly fewer hardware buttons (physical buttons on the phone). In their place is a much heavier reliance on software buttons onscreen.

In this section, I guide you through your phone's buttons.

The phone's hardware buttons

Samsung has reduced the number of hardware buttons on the Galaxy S 4 phone device. There are only three: the Power button, the Volume button, and the Home button. Before you get too far, orient yourself to be sure you're looking at the correct side of the phone. The image in Figure 2-6 shows the phone's right side.

Note: When I refer to the left or right of the phone, I'm assuming a vertical orientation, meaning you're not holding the phone sideways.

The Power button

The Power button is on right side of the phone, when you hold it in vertical orientation, toward the top.

In addition to powering up the phone, pressing the Power button puts the device into sleep mode if you press it for a moment while the phone is on.

Sleep mode shuts off the screen and suspends most running applications.

The phone automatically goes into sleep mode after about 30 seconds of inactivity to save power, but you might want to do this manually when you put away your phone. The Super AMOLED (Active-Matrix Organic Light-Emitting Diode) screen on your Samsung Galaxy S 4 is cool, but it also uses a lot of power.

Don't confuse sleep mode with powering off. Because the screen is the biggest user of power on your phone, having the screen go dark saves battery life. The phone is still alert to any incoming calls; when someone calls, the screen automatically lights up.

The Volume button (s)

Technically, there are two Volume buttons: Volume Up to increase the volume, and Volume Down to lower it. Their location is shown in Figure 2-7.

The Volume buttons control the volume of all the audio sources on the phone, including

  ✔ The phone ringer for when a call comes in
  ✔ The phone headset when you're talking on the phone
  ✔ The volume from the digital music and video player

Power button   Volume buttons

Figure 2-6: The right profile of the
Galaxy S 4.

Figure 2-7: The Galaxy S 4 Volume
buttons on the left.

The Volume controls are aware of the context of what volume you're changing. For example, if you're listening to music, adjusting volume raises or
lowers the music volume but leaves the ringer and phone earpiece volumes
unchanged.

The Volume buttons are complementary to software settings you can make
within the applications. For example, you can open the music player software
and turn up the volume on the appropriate screen. Then you can use the
hardware buttons to turn down the volume, and you'll see the volume setting
on the screen go down.

The Home button

The biggest button the phone is the Home button (see Figure 2-8). It is on the bottom of the front screen.

The Home button brings you back to the home screen from wherever you are in an application. If you are working on applications and feel like you are helplessly lost, don't worry. Press the Home button, close your eyes, tap your heels together three times, and think to yourself, "There's no place like home," and you will be brought back to the Home screen.

You don't really need to do all that other stuff after pressing the Home button. Just pressing the Home button does the trick.

The touchscreen

To cram all the information that you need onto one screen, Samsung takes the modern approach to screen layout. You'll want to become familiar with several finger navigation motions to work with your screen.

Home button

Figure 2-8: The Galaxy S 4 Home button on the front.

Before diving in, though, here's a small list of terms you need to know:

- **Icon:** This is a little image. Tapping an icon launches an application or performs some function, like making a telephone call.

- **Button:** A button on a touchscreen is meant to look like a three-dimensional button that you would push on, say, a telephone. Buttons are typically labeled to tell you what it will do when you tap it. For example, you'll see buttons labeled "Save" or "Send."

- **Hyperlink:** Sometimes called a "link," for short, a hyperlink is text that performs some function when you tap it. Usually, text is lifeless. If you tap a word and it does nothing, it's just text. If you tap a word and it launches a website or causes a screen to pop up, it's a hyperlink.

- **Thumbnail:** This is a small, low-resolution version of a larger, high-resolution picture stored somewhere else.

With this background, it's time to discuss the motions on the touchscreen you'll be using.

You need to clean the touchscreen glass from time to time. The glass on your phone is Gorilla Glass (made by Corning) and is the toughest stuff available to protect against breakage. Use a soft cloth or microfiber to get off fingerprints. You can even wipe the touchscreen on your clothes. However, never use a paper towel! Over time, glass is no match for fibers in the humble paper towel.

Tap

Often, you just tap the screen to make things happen (like launching an app) or select options. Think of a tap as a single click of a mouse on a computer screen. A tap is simply a touch of the screen, much like using a touch screen at a retail kiosk. Figure 2-9 shows what the tap motion should look like.

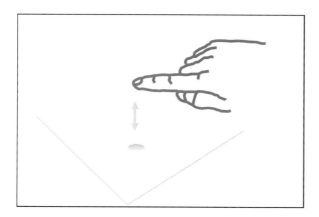

Figure 2-9: The tap motion.

One difference between a mouse click on a computer and a tap on a Galaxy S 4 phone is that a single tap launches applications on the phone in the same way that a double-click of the mouse launches an application on a computer.

A tap is different from "press and hold" (see the next section). If you leave your finger on the screen for more than an instant, the phone thinks that you want to do something other than launch an application.

Press and hold

Press and hold, as the name implies, involves putting your finger on an icon on the screen and leaving it there for more than a second. What happens when you leave your finger on an icon depends upon the situation.

For example, when you press and hold on an application on the Home screen (the screen that comes up after you turn on the phone), a garbage can icon appears on the screen. This is to remove that icon from that screen. And when you press and hold an application icon from the list of applications, the phone assumes that you want to copy that application to your Home screen. Don't worry if these distinctions might not make sense yet. The point is that you should be familiar with holding and pressing — and that it's different from tapping.

You don't need to tap or press and hold very hard for the phone to know that you want it to do something. Neither do you need to worry about breaking the glass, even by pressing on it very hard. If you hold the phone in one hand and tap with the other, you'll be fine. I suppose you might break the glass on the phone if you put it on the floor and press up into a one-fingered handstand. I don't recommend this, but if you do try it, please post the video on YouTube.

On average, a person calls 911 about once every year. Usually, you call 911 because of a stressful situation. The Samsung Galaxy S 4, like every phone, has a special stress sensor that causes it to lock up when you need it most. Okay, not really, but it seems that way. When you are stressed, it's easy to think that you are tapping when you are actually pressing and holding. Be aware of this tendency and remember to tap.

Moving around the screen or to the next screen

Additional finger motions help you move around the screens and to adjust the scaling for images that you want on the screen. Mastering these motions is important to getting the most from your phone.

The first step is navigating the screen to access what's not visible onscreen. Think of this as navigating a regular computer screen, where you use a horizontal scroll bar to access information to the right or left of what's visible on your monitor, or a vertical scroll bar to move you up and down on a screen.

The same concept works on your phone. To overcome the practical realities of screen size on a phone that will fit into your pocket, the Galaxy S 4 phone uses a panorama screen layout, meaning that you keep scrolling left or right (or maybe up and down) to access different screens.

In a nutshell, although the full width of a screen is accessible, only the part bounded by the screen of the Galaxy S 4 phone is visible on the display. Depending upon the circumstances, you have several choices on how to get to information not visible on the active screen. These actions include drag, flicks, pinch and stretch, and double taps. I cover all these in the following sections.

Drag

The simplest finger motion on the phone is the drag. You place your finger on a point on the screen and then drag the image with your finger. Then you lift your finger. Figure 2-10 shows what the drag motion looks like.

Figure 2-10: The drag motion for controlled movement.

Dragging allows you to move slowly around the panorama. This motion is like clicking a scroll bar and moving it slowly.

Flick

To move quickly around the panorama, you can flick the screen to move in the direction of your flick (see Figure 2-11).

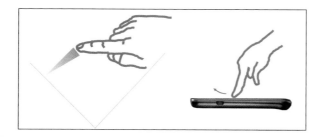

Figure 2-11: Use a flick motion for faster movement.

Better control of this motion comes with practice. In general, the faster the flick, the more the panorama moves. However, some screens, like the extended Home screen, move only one screen to the right or left no matter how fast you flick.

Pinch and stretch

Some screens allow you to change the scale of images you view on your screen. When this feature is active, the Zoom options change the magnification of the area on the screen. You can zoom out to see more features at a smaller size, or zoom in to see more detail at a larger size.

To zoom out, you put two fingers (apart) on the screen and pull them together to pinch the image. The pinch motion is shown in Figure 2-12.

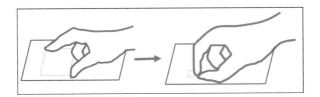

Figure 2-12: Use the pinch motion to zoom out.

The opposite motion is to zoom in. This involves the stretch motion, as shown in Figure 2-13. You place two fingers (close together) and stretch them apart. Make sure you're centered on the spot where you want to see in more detail.

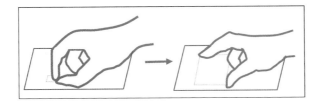

Figure 2-13: Use the stretch motion to zoom in.

Double tap

The double tap (shown in Figure 2-14) just means tapping the same button area on the screen twice in rapid succession. You use the double tap to jump between a zoomed-in and a zoomed-out image to get you back to the previous resolution. This option saves you from any frustration in getting back to a familiar perspective.

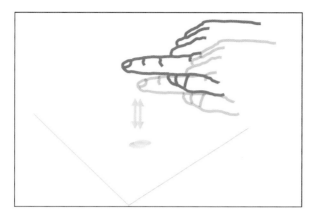

Figure 2-14: The double-tap motion.

Time the taps so that the phone doesn't interpret them as two separate taps. With a little practice, you'll master the timing of the second tap.

Air Gesture, Air View, and eye gestures

The Samsung Galaxy S 4 adds some new capabilities to the mix. These show off just how smart this phone really is!

Air View allows you to hover your finger over the screen to get a preview of what is in store for you. For example, if you have programmed some of your contacts to speed dial, you can hover your finger over a number and it will tell you to whom that speed dial number is assigned. You can also hover your finger over a web page and zoom in.

The Air Gesture capability allows you to navigate your phone without your ever having to touch it. Instead of the screen sensing your fingertips, the camera watches for your hand. If you sweep your hand over the screen to the right, the screen sweeps to the right. This also works to pan left, up, or down.

If that isn't cool enough, look at the Eye Scan feature. This capability watches where your eyes are reading on the screen. When it reaches the bottom, the phone assumes that you want to continue and automatically scrolls down and brings up more of the page.

The next eye gesture is called *SmartPause*. If you are watching a video and look away, the phone automatically pauses the video for you. When you look back, it resumes playing and picks up where you left off. Now your phone has one up on your HD TV!

TIP

SmartPause takes some getting used to. Many of us have become so used to missing pieces of a video that when it pauses unexpectedly, it's distracting. You can turn off this capability by tapping the On/Off button in Settings➪Display➪SmartPause.

The extended Home screen

The extended Home screen (just Home screen, for short) is the first screen that you see when the phone is done setting up. Samsung has set it to be five screen-widths wide and one screen high.

Figure 2-15 shows a representation of the full Home screen layout. At any given moment, of course, you see only one screen at a time.

The extended Home screen is where you can organize icons and other functions to make the phone convenient for you. Out of the box, Samsung and your cellular carrier have worked together to create a starting point for you. Beyond that, though, you have lots of ways that you can customize your Home screen so that you have easy access to the things that are most important for you. Much of the book covers all the things that the phone can do, but a recurring theme is how to put that capability on your Home screen if you wish.

To start, check out the layout of the Home screen and how it relates to other areas of the phone. Knowing these areas is important for basic navigation.

Figure 2-16 shows a typical Home screen and highlights three important areas on the phone.

Figure 2-15: The Galaxy S 4 phone panorama display of the extended Home screen.

Figure 2-16: Important areas on the Galaxy S 4 phone and Home screen.

✔ **The notification area:** This part of the screen presents you with small icons that let you know if something important is up, like battery life.

✔ **The primary shortcuts:** These five icons remain stationary as you move across the home screen. Samsung and your cellular carrier have determined that these are the five most important applications on your phone.

✔ **The Device Function keys:** These three keys control essential phone functions, regardless of what else is going on at the moment with the phone.

There are a series of dots just above the primary shortcuts on the extended home screen. You may also notice that one of the dots isn't just a dot — it is a little house icon. That is the "home" Home screen. The largest dot indicates where you are among the screens. You can navigate among the screens by dragging the screen to the left or right. This moves you one screen at a time. You can also jump multiple screens by tapping on the dot that corresponds to the screen number you want to see, or by dragging the dots to the screen you want to see. Keep reading for more detail on each area.

Adding shortcuts to the Home Screen

As seen in Figure 2-15, you have a lot of screen real estate where you can put icons of your favorite applications and widgets (widgets are small apps that take care of simple functions, like displaying time or the status of your battery). You can add shortcuts to the apps and these widgets to your Home screen by following these steps:

1. **From the extended Home screen, tap the Menu button.**

   This brings up a pop-up at the bottom of the screen, as shown in Figure 2-17.

2. **Tap the Add Apps and Widgets button.**

   The screen shown in Figure 2-18 appears. It either displays all the icons of all the apps you currently have on your phone or it shows all the widgets you currently have on your phone. The screen in Figure 2-18 shows the apps. You can see all the apps by sliding around the apps screens.

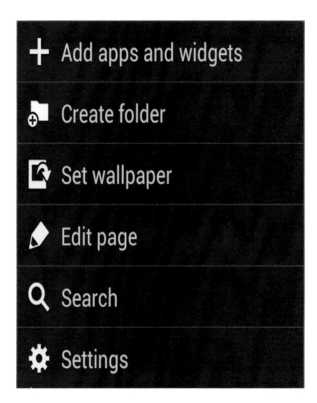

+ Add apps and widgets

Create folder

Set wallpaper

Edit page

Q Search

Settings

Figure 2-17: The Menu pop-up from the Home screen.

Figure 2-18: The apps you can add to your Home screen.

If you want to see widgets instead, tap on the word *Widget* towards the top of the screen. It appears slightly grayed out. This takes to you the Widgets screen, like the ones seen in Figure 2-19. Slide your finger across the screen to bring up the different Widgets screens.

3. Press and Hold on the Icon you want.

After you see the app or widget you want to appear on your Home screen, press and hold the icon.

In a few seconds, the app or widget appears on the Home screen you were on most recently. Done.

Taking away shortcuts

Say that you put the shortcut on the wrong screen. No problem. You can press and hold it, and then drag it left or right until it's on the screen you want. Taking a shortcut off your Home screen is simple. Press and hold the shortcut on the screen. In a moment, a garbage can icon appears at the top of the screen. Drag the doomed shortcut to the garbage can, and off it goes to its maker.

It is gone, but if you made a mistake, you can get it back easily enough. To re-create it, simply go back to the App Menu key and follow the process again.

The notification area and screen

As shown in Figure 2-16, the notification area is located at the top of the phone. Here, you see little status icons. Maybe you received a text or an e-mail, or you'll see an application needs some tending to.

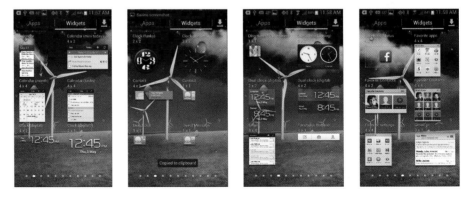

Figure 2-19: The Widgets screens with the widgets you can add to your Home screen.

Think of the notification area as a special e-mail inbox where your carrier (or even the phone itself) can give you important information about what's happening with your phone. The large icons at the top tell you the condition of the different radio systems on your phone: The number of bars shown gives you an indication of signal strength, and the phone also usually tells you what kind of signal you're getting – like 3G or 4G.

You could take the time to learn the meanings of all the little icons that might come up, but that would take you a while. A more convenient option is to touch the notification area and drag it down, shown in Figure 2-20.

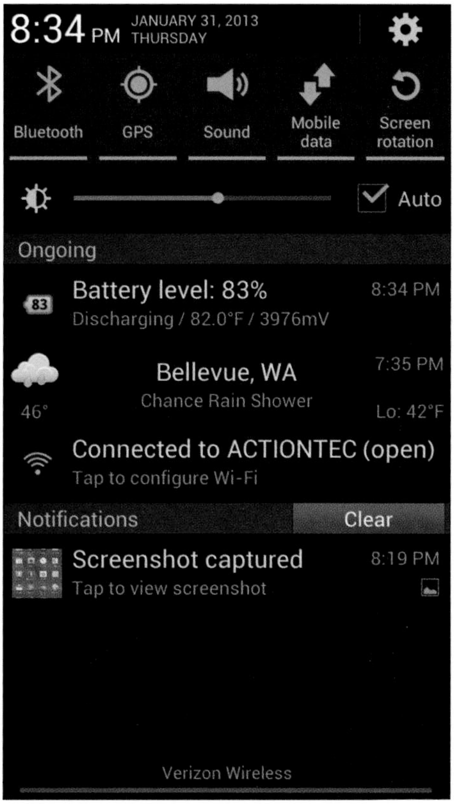

Figure 2-20: Pay attention to the notification screen for important events.

The rest of the screen is written so that you can understand what's going on — and what, if anything, you're expected to do. For example, if you see that you have a new e-mail, you tap the text of the link, and you're taken to your new e-mail.

When you're finished reading the notifications, you slide your finger back up to the top. You can also clear this screen if it gets too full by tapping the Clear button. You can also clear notifications one at a time by touching them and swiping them to the side.

The primary shortcuts

The primary shortcuts are what Samsung and your cellular carrier decided on as the five most important functions of your phone. Each phone type has its own twist on this, but all phones sport a phone icon so that making calls is fast and convenient.

Among the other possible shortcuts here are shortcuts that take you to your contacts, your e-mail, the Internet, texting/messaging, or your list of applications. These shortcuts are not customizable. Don't worry, though. This is not much of a limitation.

The Device Function keys

At the bottom of the screen, below the rectangular screen displays, are three important buttons, the Device Function keys. They're always present for you to navigate your phone even though the backlight might switch off to hide their presence. Whatever else you're doing on the phone, these buttons can take over.

The button on the left of the Home button is the Menu key. Tapping it brings up a list of options you can select. The key to the right of the Home button is a Return key. If it is lit, you can tap it and it will take you back one step.

The Device Function keys are kind of cool because they light up when you are touching them or the screen, and fade away the rest of the time.

The Menu button

Tapping the Menu button brings up a pop-up menu at the bottom of the screen from which you can access valuable capabilities. What's "valuable" depends upon what application is running at that time. For example, in Figure 2-17, you can see the options you can select from the Home screen.

The Home button

As I discussed earlier, pressing the Home button takes you directly to the extended Home screen.

The Home button comes in handy when you want to change what you're doing with the phone, such as going from browsing the web to making a phone call. I talk about a cool capability secretly enabled with this button in Chapter 15.

The Back button

The Back button on your phone is similar to the Back button in a web browser: It takes you back one screen.

As you start navigating through the screens on your phone, pressing the Back button takes you back to the previous screen. If you keep pressing the Back button, you'll eventually return to the Home screen.

The keyboard

The screen of the Galaxy S 4 phone is important, but you'll still probably spend more time on the keyboard entering data on the QWERTY keyboard.

Using the software keyboard

The software keyboard automatically pops up when the application detects a need for user text input. The keyboard appears at the bottom of the screen.

For example, say you're in Seattle, searching for the Seattle Art Museum via the Mapping application. Tap the Search button, and the keyboard pops up onscreen, as shown in Figure 2-21.

In this case, a text box pops up in addition to the keyboard. As you type **Seattle Art Museum**, the text appears in the box on the screen as if you had typed it on a hardware keyboard. The phone is smart enough to know when the keyboard should appear and disappear. If the keyboard doesn't appear when you want to start typing, you can tap on the text box where you want to enter data.

Using Swype

Galaxy S 4 phones come with an enhanced data-entering capability called Swype. This option automatically comes with your phone, and with a little practice, can dramatically speed your ability to type fast on your phone.

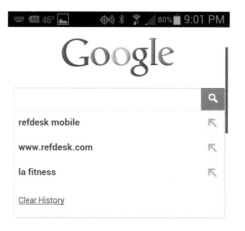

Keyboard pop-up

Figure 2-21: Use the software keyboard to enter data.

Here's how Swype works: Instead of tapping each discrete key on the keyboard, you leave your finger on the screen and swipe from key to key. The Swype application figures out the words you are wanting to type, including inserting the spaces automatically.

If you like Swype, you can use it any time that you're entering data. If you don't care for it, you can just tap your letters. It's all up to you!

Using Voice Recognition

The third option for a keyboard is . . . no keyboard at all! Galaxy S 4 phones come with the option of having voice recognition. It is very easy, and works surprisingly well. In most spots where you have an option to enter text, you see a small version of the following logo.

Just tap on this icon and say what you would have typed. You see the phone thinking for a second, and then it shows a screen that looks like Figure 2-22.

When you are done, you can tap the "done" button, or just be quiet. Within a few seconds, you will see what you said!

Figure 2-22: The Voice Recognition screen.

The orientation of the phone

In the earlier section where I discuss the Power button, I referred to the phone being in vertical orientation (so that the phone is tall and narrow). It can also be used in the landscape orientation (sideways, or so that the phone is short and wide). The phone senses which direction you're holding the phone and orients the screen to make it easier for you to view.

The phone makes its orientation known to the application, but not all applications are designed to change their inherent display. That nuance is left to the writers of the application. For example, your phone can play videos. However, the video player application that comes with your phone shows video in landscape mode only.

In addition, the phone can sense when you are holding it to you ear. When it senses that it is held in this position, it shuts off the screen. You need not be concerned that you will accidentally "chin dial" a number in Botswana.

Going to Sleep Mode/Turning Off the Phone

You can leave your phone on every minute until you're ready to upgrade to the newest Galaxy S 4 phone in a few years, but that will use up your battery in no time. Instead, put your idle phone in sleep mode to save battery power. *Note:* This also happens automatically after 30 seconds of inactivity on the screen.

You can adjust the screen timeout for a longer duration, which I cover in Chapter 16. Or, you can manually put the phone in sleep mode by pressing the Power button for just a moment.

Sometimes it's best to simply shut down the phone if you aren't going to use it for several days or more. To shut down the phone completely, simply press and hold the Power button for a few seconds. The following options appear:

- **Silent mode:** Turn off sound.
- **Airplane mode:** Turns off the radios that communicate to the local Wi-Fi access point and the cellular network so that you can't receive or make voice calls or send or receive texts or data. As the name implies, use this setting when you're flying, but you want to use applications that can operate without a data connection, such as some games or e-mail. Because some flights now provide Wi-Fi, the phone *does* allow you to turn Wi-Fi back on when you're in airplane mode if you need it.
- **Power Off:** Shut down the phone completely.

Good night!

Part II
Communications

Visit www.dummies.com/extras/samsunggalaxys4 for tips on how to add a contact from a text.

In this part . . .

- Dialing and answering phone calls
- Connecting to a Bluetooth headset
- Sending and receiving text messages
- Setting up e-mail accounts on your phone
- Getting all your contacts in one location

Calling People

In This Chapter

▷ Dialing and answering phone calls

▷ Using your call list

▷ Making emergency calls

▷ Connecting to a Bluetooth headset

*A*t its essence, any cellphone — no matter how fancy or smart — exists to make phone calls. The good news is that making and receiving phone calls on your Galaxy S 4 is easy.

In this chapter, I show you how not only how to make a call but how to use your call list to keep track of your calls. And don't skip the section on using your phone for emergencies.

Finally, if you're like many people, you're never doing just one thing at a time, and a Bluetooth headset can make it easier for you to talk on the phone while driving, wrangling kids and dogs, or just plain living life. In this chapter, I show you how to hook up your phone to a Bluetooth headset so you can make and receive phone calls hands-free.

Making Calls

After your phone is on and you're connected to your cellular carrier (see Chapters 1 and 2), you can make a phone call. It all starts from the Home screen. Along the bottom of the screen, above the Device Function keys, are five icons, which are the *primary shortcuts* (see Figure 3-1). *Note:* From left to right, they are

- ✔ Phone
- ✔ Contacts
- ✔ Messaging
- ✔ Internet
- ✔ Apps

Primary shortcuts

Figure 3-1: The primary shortcuts on the Home screen.

To make a call, follow these steps:

1. **From the Home screen, tap the Phone icon.**

   The Keypad screen (see Figure 3-2) appears. This looks like a stylized version of a touch pad on a regular landline phone.

2. **Tap the telephone number you want to call.**

   Don't be alarmed if you don't hear a dial tone until you tap Send; smartphones don't connect to a network and start a dial tone until after you dial your number.

   For long distance calls while in the U.S., you don't need to dial 1 before the area code — just dial the area code and then the seven-digit phone number. Similarly, you can include the "1" and the area code for local calls. On the other hand, if you are traveling internationally, you need to include the "1" and be prepared for international roaming charges!

   In Chapter 5, you can read about how to make a phone call through your contacts.

3. **Tap the green Send button at the bottom of the screen to place the call.**

   Within a few seconds, you should hear the phone ringing at the other end or a busy signal.

4. **When you're done with your call, tap the End button — the red button at the bottom of the screen.**

   The call is disconnected.

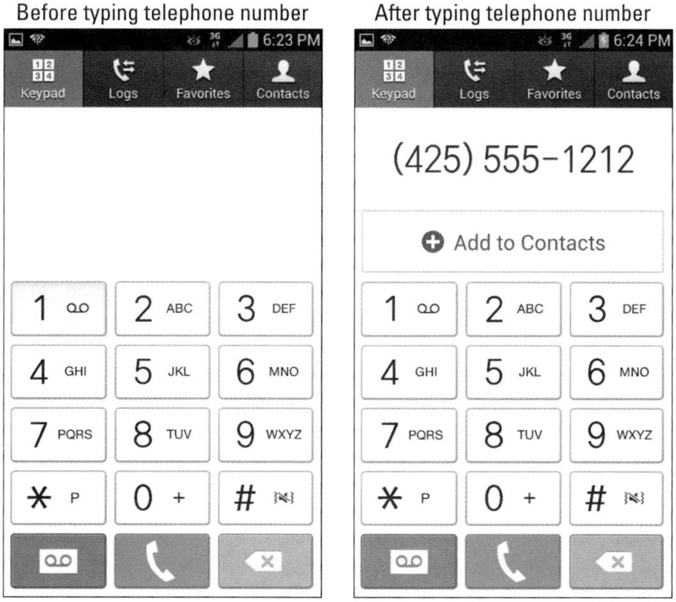

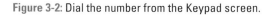

Figure 3-2: Dial the number from the Keypad screen.

If the call doesn't go through, either the cellular coverage where you are is insufficient, or your phone got switched to Airplane mode. It is possible that your cellular carrier let you out of the door without having set you up for service, but that's pretty unlikely!

Check the notification section of your phone at the top of the screen. If there are no connection strength bars, try moving to another location. If you see a small plane silhouette, bring down the notification screen (see how in Chapter 2) and tap the plane icon to turn off Airplane mode.

If you pull down the notification screen and do not see the green silhouette of an airplane, scroll the green or gray icons to the left. This icon may be off the page. Alternatively, tap the icon with the boxes in the upper-right corner and you will see all the notification icons, as shown in Figure 3-3.

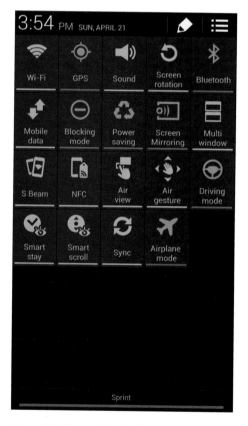

Figure 3-3: The notification icons.

Answering Calls

Receiving a call is even easier than making a call. When someone calls you, caller ID information appears along with three icons. Figure 3-4 shows a typical screen for an incoming call.

Figure 3-4: The screen when you're receiving a call.

To answer the call, put your finger on the green phone icon and slide it to the right. To not answer a call, you can simply ignore the ringing or you can put your finger on the red phone icon and slide it to the left. The ringing stops immediately. In either case, the call will go to voicemail.

In Part IV, I fill you in on some exciting options that you can enable (or not) when you get a call. For example, you can specify a unique ringtone for a particular number, or have an image of the caller pop up onscreen (if you save your contacts to your phone).

Regardless of what you were doing on the phone at that moment — such as listening to music or playing a game — the answer screen can appear. Any active application, including music or video, is suspended until the call is over.

You must set up your voicemail for callers to leave you messages. If you haven't yet set up your voicemail, the caller will hear a recorded message saying that your voicemail account isn't yet set up. Some cellular carriers can set up voicemail for you when you activate the account and get the phone; others require you to set up voicemail on your own. Ask how voicemail works at your carrier store or look for instructions in the manual included with your phone.

These two main buttons are pretty standard on any cellular phone. However, your Galaxy S 4 is no standard phone. There is a third option, and what happens depends upon your individual phone.

In addition to the standard options of Answer (a green phone facing up) and Ignore (a red phone facing down) buttons when a call comes in, you have one more option — to ignore *and* send the caller a text message. Assuming that your caller is sent to your voicemail, you also can automatically send the caller a text message that acknowledges the call.

Some of the typical "canned" messages that you can send are

- I'm driving.
- I'm at the cinema.
- I'm in class now.
- I'm in a meeting.
- Sorry, I'm busy. Call back later.

You tap the message that applies. The message is sent as a text right away, which alerts the caller that you're not ignoring him — it's just that you can't talk right now. Nice touch.

You can also create and store your own message, like "Go away and leave me alone," or "Whatever I am doing is more important than talking to you." You could also be polite. To create your own canned message, tap the "Create New Message" and type away. It's then stored on your phone for when you need it.

The caller has to be able to receive text messages. This feature doesn't work if your caller is calling from a landline or a cellphone that can't receive texts.

Keeping Track of Your Calls: The Call List

One of the nice features of cellular phones is that the phone keeps a record of the calls that you've made and received. Sure, you might have caller ID on your landline at home or work, but most landline phones don't keep track of who you called. Cellphones, on the other hand, keep track of all the numbers you called. This information can be very convenient, like when you want to return a call, and you don't have that number handy. In addition, you can easily add a number to the contact list on your phone.

By tapping the "Recent" icon, you get a list of all incoming and outgoing calls. (This icon, located at the top of the screen, is a phone receiver with arrows pointing to it and away; see Figure 3-2.) Each call bears an icon telling you whether it was an

- **Outgoing call you made:** An orange arrow points to the number.
- **Incoming call you received:** A green arrow points away from the number.
- **Incoming call you missed:** A red phone silhouette with a broken arrow.
- **Incoming call you ignored:** A blue slash sign is next to the phone icon.

A typical call log is shown in Figure 3-5.

By tapping any number in your call list, you see a screen like the one shown in Figure 3-6. From this screen, you can do several things:

- See the date and time the call was logged and all previous calls to and from this number.
- Call the number by tapping the green call button. There is an even easier option that I describe in the nearby sidebar, "Samsung Galaxy S 4 for lazy bones: Direct Call."
- Send a text to that number by tapping the number and then tapping Send Message on the pop-up screen that appears. (More on this in Chapter 4.)
- Mark that number as a favorite by tapping the star icon. Your favorites appear on the Keypad screen (refer to Figure 3-2), which saves you from having to dial those numbers.
- Add the number to your contacts list by tapping the "Create Contact" button. A pop-up gives you the option to add it to you contacts, either by creating a new contact or adding to an existing one. I cover contacts more in Chapter 6.

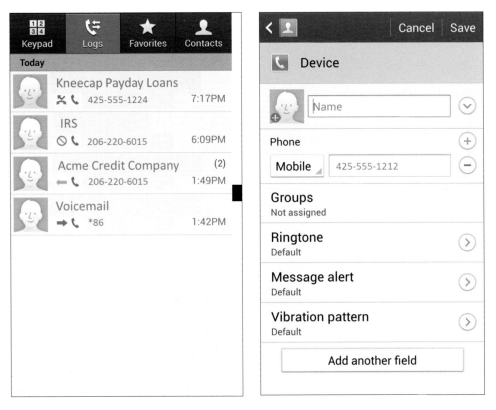

Figure 3-5: A call log.

Figure 3-6: A call log contact.

Making an Emergency Call: The 411 on 911

Cellphones are wonderful tools for calling for help in an emergency. The Samsung Galaxy S 4, like all phones in the United States and Canada, can make emergency calls to 911.

Just tap the Phone icon on the Home screen, tap **911**, and then tap Send. You'll be routed to the 911 call center nearest to your location. This works wherever you are within the United States. So, say you live in Chicago but have a car accident in Charlotte; just tap 911 to be connected to the 911 call center in Charlotte, not Chicago.

Samsung Galaxy S 4 for lazy bones: Direct Call

Imagine this scenario. You show up to work, and two co-workers have called in sick. You spend your day hustling to cover for them. You get home and clean the house. It has snowed, so you need to shovel your walk and driveway, as well as for the elderly widow next door. (You are that kind of person.)

All you want to do is flop down on the sofa and pick up your Samsung Galaxy S 4 to call your best friend. You find them in the call log, but pure exhaustion kicks in, and you just don't have

it in you to tap that green phone icon to start the dialing process.

No need to worry. Your Samsung Galaxy S 4 has taken care of you. Simply put the phone to your ear! After a moment, the phone gives a quick shake and the phone automatically dials that number for you.

Samsung calls this capability *Direct Call*. Using this feature requires an exceptional level of laziness, which is why I am so fond of it!

Even if your phone isn't registered on a network, you don't have a problem. You phone lets you know that the only number you can dial is a 911 call center.

When you call 911 from a landline, the address you're calling from is usually displayed for the operator. When you're calling from a cellphone, though, the operator doesn't have that specific information. So, when you call 911, the operator might say, "911. *Where* is your emergency?" Don't let this question throw you; after all, you're probably focused on *what* is happening and not on *where*. Take a moment and come up with a good description of where you are — the street you're on, the nearest cross street (if you know it), any businesses or other landmarks nearby. When the operator knows where you are, she's in a better position to help you with your emergency. Your phone does have a GPS receiver in it that 911 centers can access. However, it is not always accurate as it may not be receiving location information at the moment, such as when you are indoors.

When traveling outside the United States or Canada, 911 might not be the number you call in an emergency. Mexico uses 066, 060, or 080, but most tourist areas also accept 911. And most of — but not all of — Europe uses 112. Knowing the local emergency number is as important as knowing the language.

When you accidentally dial 911

If you accidentally dial 911 from your phone, don't hang up. Just tell the operator that it was an accidental call. She might ask some questions to verify that you are indeed safe and not being forced to say that your call was an accident.

If you panic and hang up after accidentally dialing 911, you'll get a call from the nearest 911 call center. Always answer the call, even if you feel foolish. If you don't answer the call, the 911 call centers will assume that you're in trouble and can't respond. They'll track you down from the GPS in your phone to verify that you're safe. If you thought you'd feel foolish explaining your mistake to a 911 operator, imagine how foolish you'd feel explaining it to the police officer who tracks you down and is upset with you for wasting their time.

Synching a Bluetooth Headset

With a Bluetooth headset device, you can talk on your phone without needing to hold the phone and without any cords running from the phone to your earpiece. You've probably come across plenty of people talking on Bluetooth headsets. You might even have wondered whether they were a little crazy, talking to themselves. Well, call yourself crazy now, because when you start using a Bluetooth headset, you might never want to go back.

Not surprisingly, Galaxy S 4 phones can connect to Bluetooth devices. The first step to using a Bluetooth headset with your phone is to sync the two devices. Here's how:

1. **From the Home screen on your phone, tap the Apps icon.**

   This gets you to the list of all the applications on your phone.

2. **Flick or pan to the Settings icon and tap it.**

   The Settings icon is shown here. This screen holds most of the settings that you can adjust on your phone.

Tapping on the Settings icon brings up the screen seen in Figure 3-7.

3. **Tap the Bluetooth Off button to toggle it to On.**

   Be careful not to tap the green button to the right of the Bluetooth icon and title if it is set to On. This would turn off Bluetooth. That defeats the purpose.

4. **Tap the Bluetooth icon.**

   This brings up Figure 3-8.

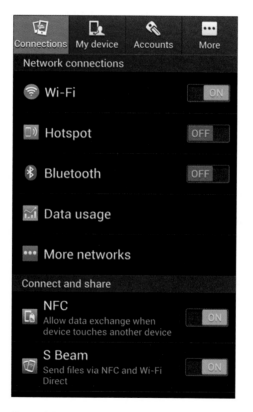

Figure 3-7: The Settings screen.

5. **Tap the box to the right of the title of your Phone's model number.**

   This enables your phone to be visible to other Bluetooth devices. This state will last for 120 seconds. That is enough time for you to get your Bluetooth device also into pairing mode so they can negotiate the proper security settings and pair up every time they "see" each other going forward.

6. **Tap the bar at the bottom with the word Scan.**

Your phone scans the area for other Bluetooth devices.

7. **Put your headset into synching mode.**

Follow the instructions that came with your headset.

After a moment, the phone "sees" the headset. When it does, you are prompted to enter the security code, and the software keyboard pops up.

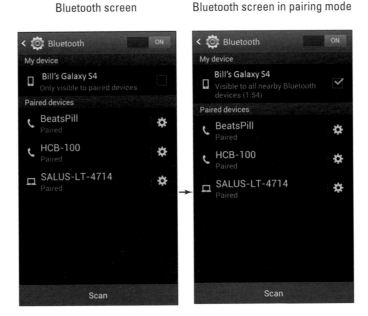

Figure 3-8: The Bluetooth Settings screen.

8. **Enter the security code for your headset and then tap the Enter button.**

The security code on most headsets is 0000, but check the instructions that came with your headset if that number doesn't work.

Your phone might see other devices in the immediate area. If so, it asks you which device you want to pair with. Tap the name of your headset.

Your headset is now synched to your phone. If you turn one on when the other is already on, they recognize each other and automatically pair up.

Discovering the Joy of Text

In This Chapter

▶ Sending a text message

▶ Sending a text message with an attachment

▶ Receiving a text message

Sure, cellphones are made for talking. But these days, many people use their cellphones even more for texting. *Text messages* (short messages, usually 160 characters or less, sent by cellphone) are particularly convenient when you can't talk at the moment (maybe you're in a meeting or class) or when you just have a small bit of information to share ("Running late — see you soon!").

Many cellphone users — particularly younger ones — prefer sending texts to making a phone call. They find texting a faster and more convenient way to communicate, and they often use texting shorthand to fit more "content" in that character limit.

Even the most basic phones support texting these days, but your Galaxy S 4 phone makes sending and receiving text messages more convenient, no matter whether you're an occasional or pathological texter. In this chapter, I fill you in on how to send a text message (with or without an attachment), how to receive a text message, and how to read your old text messages.

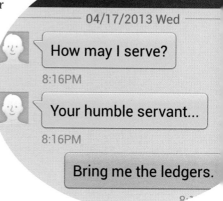

To use text messaging, you must have texting capability as part of your service plan. See Chapter 1 for more info.

Sending the First Text Message

There are two scenarios for texting. The first is when you send someone a text for the first time. The second is when you have a text conversation with a person.

When you first get your phone and are ready to brag about your new Galaxy S 4 and want to send a text to your best friend, here's how easy it is:

1. **On the Home screen, tap the Messaging icon.**

The Messaging application is between the contacts and the Internet icons. When you tap it, you will get a mostly blank home texting screen. This is shown in Figure 4-1.

When you have some conversations going, it begins to fill up. More on that soon.

2. **Tap the New Message icon (the pencil hovering over a blank page).**

Tapping the New Message icon brings up the screen seen in Figure 4-2.

3. **Tap to enter the ten-digit mobile telephone number of the recipient.**

A text box appears at the top of the screen with the familiar To field at the top. The keyboard appears at the bottom of the screen.

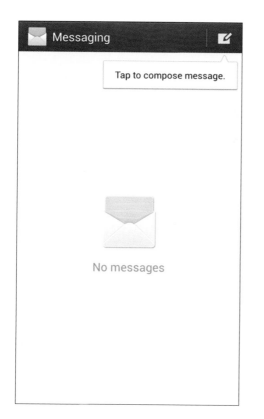

Figure 4-1: The Messaging Home screen.

Figure 4-2: A blank texting screen.

As shown in Figure 4-3, the top field is where you type in the telephone number. The numerals are along the top of the keyboard.

Be sure to include the area code, even if the person you are texting is local. However, there is no need to put a "1" before the number.

If this is your first text, you haven't had a chance to build up a history of texts. After you've been using your messaging application for a while, you will have entered contact information.

4. **To write your text message, tap the text box that says Enter Message. Figure 4-4 shows you where to enter your text.**

Your text message can be up to 160 characters, including spaces and punctuation. The application counts down the number of characters you have left.

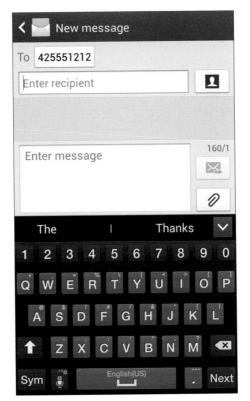

Figure 4-3: Type the recipient's number in the upper text box.

Type your message here.

Recipient's number

Figure 4-4: Type your text here.

5. **Send the text by tapping the Send button to the right of your message.**

   The Send button is the one with the image of an envelope with the arrow on it. The phone takes it from here. Within a few seconds, the message is sent to your friend's cellphone.

After you build your contact list (read about this in Chapter 6), you can tap a name from the contact list or start typing a name in the recipient text box. If there's only one number for that contact, your phone assumes that's the receiving phone you want to send a text to. If that contact has multiple numbers, it asks you which phone number you want to send your text to.

You've probably heard a thousand times about how it is a very bad idea to text while you are driving. Here comes one-thousand-and-one. It is a *very bad idea* to text while you are driving — and illegal in some places. There are Dummies who read this book (and are actually very smart), and then there are DUMMIES who text and drive. I want you to be the former and not the latter.

Carrying on a Conversation via Texting

In the bad ol' pre-Galaxy S days, most cellular phones would keep a log of your texts. The phone would keep each text that you sent or received in sequential order, regardless of who sent or received them.

Texts stored sequentially are old-school. Your Galaxy S 4 keeps track of the contact with which you have been texting and puts it into a "conversation."

In Figure 4-5, you can see that the first page for messaging refers to *conversations.* After you start texting someone, those texts are stored in one conversation.

As Figure 4-5 shows, each text message is presented in sequence, with the author of the text indicated by the direction of the text balloon.

Note the Type to Compose text box at the bottom of the screen. With this convenient feature, you can send whatever you type to the person with whom you're having a conversation.

In the bad old days, it was sometimes hard to keep straight the different texting conversations you were having. When you start a texting conversation with someone else, there is a second conversation.

Before too long, you will have multiple conversations going on. Don't worry. It isn't the kind of conversation where you need to keep the conversation going. No one thinks twice if you do not text for a while. The image in Figure 4-6 shows how the text page from Figure 4-1 can look before too long.

Figure 4-5: A messaging conversation.

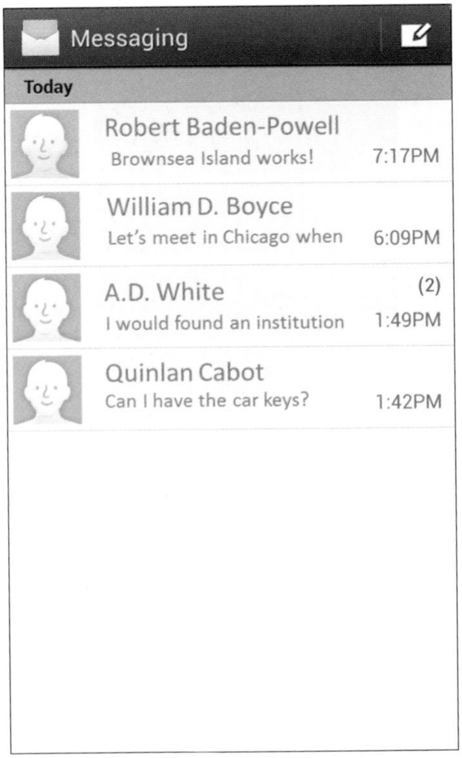

Figure 4-6: The Text screen showing multiple conversations.

Sending an Attachment with a Text

What if you want to send something in addition to or instead of text? Say, you want to send a picture, some music, or a Word document along with your text. Easy as pie, as long as the phone on the receiving end can recognize the attachment. Here is the recipe:

1. **From the Home screen, tap the Messaging icon.**

2. **Either tap the New Message icon and enter the number of the intended recipient, or pick up on an existing conversion.**

   You'll see the text creation page from Figure 4-3. Enter the information you want like a normal text.

3. **To add an attachment, tap the icon that looks like a paper clip.**

   The paper clip icon brings up the screen you see in Figure 4-7.

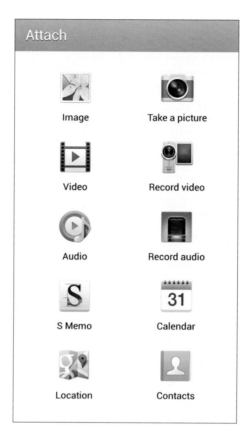

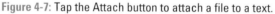

Figure 4-7: Tap the Attach button to attach a file to a text.

4. **Tap your file type choice, and your phone presents you with the options that fall into that category.**

   This asks what kind of file you want to attach. Your choices include pictures, videos, audio files, and some others I will describe later. For now, it's just good that you know that you have options.

   After you select the file, it becomes an attachment to your text message.

5. **Continue typing your text message, if needed.**

6. **When you're done with the text portion of the message, tap the Send Text button, and off it all goes.**

A simple text message is an SMS (short message service) message. When you add an attachment, you're sending an MMS (multimedia messaging service) message. Back in the day, MMS messages cost more to send and receive than SMS messages did. These days, that isn't the case in the United States.

Receiving Text Messages

Receiving a text is even easier than sending one.

When you're having a text conversation and you receive a new text from the person you're texting with, your phone signals that you have a message. It beeps, or vibrates if you have the sound off. Also, the notification area of the screen (the very top) indicates that you have a text by showing a very small version of the messaging icon.

You can either pull down the notification screen from the very top of the screen or start the messaging application. Your choice.

If an attachment comes along, it's included in the conversation screens.

To access the text, you need to unlock the screen. The Messaging icon, an envelope, also displays the number of new texts that you have. Tap that icon to open the conversations.

Managing Your Text History

The Messaging Conversations screen stores and organizes all your texts until you delete them. You should clean up this screen every now and then.

The simplest option for managing your messages is to tap the Menu icon and then tap Delete Threads. You can then select and unselect all the conversations that you want deleted. Tap the Delete link at the bottom of the screen, and they disappear.

Practice good texting hygiene. Regularly clear out older texts. It's highly unlikely that you need to keep 200 texts from anyone. Starting a new conversation is easy enough, anyway.

Another deletion option is to open the conversation. You can delete each text by pressing and holding on the balloon. After a moment, a menu appears from which you can delete that message. This method is a lot slower if you have lots of texts, though.

I recommend you be vicious in deleting the older texts and conversations. Trust me; deleting all your messages can be cathartic!

Sending and Receiving E-Mail

In This Chapter

▶ Setting up e-mail accounts on your phone

▶ Reading e-mail on your phone

▶ Managing your e-mail folder

▶ Sending e-mail from your phone

*I*f you've had e-mail on your phone for a while, you know how convenient it is. If your Galaxy S 4 phone is your first cellphone with the capability to send and receive e-mail, prepare to be hooked.

I start this chapter by showing you how to set up your e-mail, regardless of whether your e-mail is supported (more on that in a bit). Then I show you how to read and manage your e-mails. Finally, I tell you how to write and send e-mails.

Your phone primarily interacts with your inbox on your e-mail account. It isn't really set up to work like the full-featured e-mail application on your computer, though. For example, many e-mail packages integrate with a sophisticated word processor, have sophisticated filing systems for your saved messages, and offer an extensive selection of fonts. As long as you do not mind working without these advanced capabilities, you might never need to get on your computer to access your e-mail again, and you could store e-mails in folders on your phone. However, the phone access to e-mail is best used in working with the e-mails that are in your inbox.

.ail Alert [National]
 heLadders
Bill's "National" Email Alert Cre...

We need your expert opi...
TravelSupermarket.com
If you're having problems viewi...

Enjoy a Florida Spring br...
CLUB WYNDHAM
Florida is perfect for Spring Bre...

⌐0 gift card for your fa...
 ~ber Servic...

Using e-mail on your phone requires a data connection. Some cellular carriers solve this problem by obliging you to have a data plan with your phone. If your cellular carrier does not, you won't be able to use e-mail unless you're connected to a Wi-Fi hotspot. I recommend that you get that data plan and enjoy the benefits of wireless e-mail.

The advantages of getting a Gmail account

You might already have a work and a personal e-mail account. You might even have an old e-mail account that you check only once in a while because some friends, for whatever reason, haven't updated their profile for you and continue to use an old address.

The thought of getting yet another e-mail address, even one that's free, might (understandably) be unappealing. After all, it's another address and password to remember. However, some important functions on your phone require that you have a Gmail account. These include

✔ The ability to buy applications from the Play Store. (This is huge!) I go over the Play Store in Chapter 8.

✔ Free access to the photo site Picasa (although other sites have many of the same features). I cover Picasa and photo options in Chapter 9.

✔ Access to the Music and Video Hub. These slick services are explained in Chapter 12.

✔ Automatic backup of your contacts and calendar. That's explained in more detail in Chapters 6 and 13.

To make a long story short, it's worth the trouble to get a Gmail account, even if you already have a personal e-mail account.

Setting Up Your E-Mail

Your phone can manage up to ten e-mail accounts from the Email app on your phone. With a Galaxy S 4 phone (unlike some other phones), you may need to create a separate e-mail account just for your phone. However, you will miss out on so many exciting capabilities, that I highly recommend setting up a new Gmail account if you don't have one already (more on that later). You need a Gmail account to access the Google Play Store that you use to download new applications for your phone. A Gmail account is also the means to back up your contacts and calendar and it offers access to sharing photos. Without a Gmail account, you miss out on many of the best features on the Galaxy S 4.

The Email app on your phone routinely polls all the e-mail systems for which you give an e-mail account and password. It then presents you with a copy of your e-mails.

Setup is so easy and makes you so productive that I advise you to consider adding all your e-mail accounts to your phone.

Getting ready

In general, connecting to a personal e-mail account simply involves entering the name of your e-mail account and its password in your phone. Have these handy when you are ready to set up your phone.

These days, many of us have multiple personal e-mail address for many reasons. Just have the e-mail account and password ready, and you can add all of them. You do need to pick one account as your favorite. Although you can send an e-mail using any of the accounts, your phone wants to know the e-mail account that you want it to use as a default.

Next, you may want to have access to your work account. This is relatively common these days, but some companies see this as a security problem. You should consult with your IT department for some extra information. Technologically, it is not hard to make this kind of thing happen as long as your business e-mail is reasonably modern.

Finally, if you do not already have a Gmail account, I strongly encourage you to get one. Read the nearby sidebar, "The advantages of getting a Gmail account" to find out why.

Setting up your existing Gmail account

If you already have a Gmail account, setup is easy as can be. Follow these steps from the Apps menu:

1. **Find the Gmail icon in the Apps list.**

   Here is the most confusing part. The icon on the left in Figure 5-1 is the Gmail app. The icon on the right is the icon for all your other e-mail accounts.

Figure 5-1: The Mail icons in the Apps list.

2. **Tap the Gmail icon.**

   Because your phone does not know if you have a Gmail account, it asks you whether this is a new account, as shown in Figure 5-2.

3. **Tap the Existing button on the screen.**

   This brings up the screen in Figure 5-3.

4. **Enter your existing Gmail user ID and password.**

   Go ahead and type your e-mail account address and your password. When you are ready, tap Done on the keyboard.

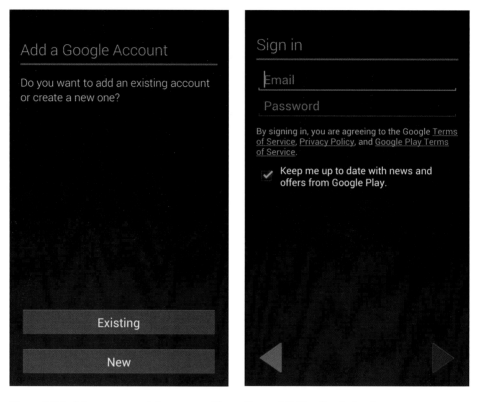

Figure 5-2: Is this a new or existing account?   Figure 5-3: The Gmail sign-in screen.

You may get a pop-up re-confirming that you agree with the terms of use and all that legal stuff. Tap OK. You'll see lots of flashing lights and whirling circles while your phone and your Gmail account get to know each other.

If everything is correct, your phone and your account get acquainted and become best friends. After a few minutes, they are ready to serve your needs. If you have a problem, you probably mistyped something. Try retyping your information in again.

From this point on, any e-mail you get on your Gmail account will also appear on your phone!

Setting up a new Gmail account

If you need to set up a new Gmail account, you have a few more steps to follow. Before I get into the steps, think up a good user ID and password.

Gmail has been around for a while. That means all the good, simple e-mail addresses are taken. Unless you plan to start using this e-mail account as your primary e-mail, which you could do if you wanted, you are probably best off if you pick some unusual combination of letters and numbers that you can remember for now to get through this process.

When you have this ready, follow Steps 1 and 2 in the previous section, but tap New instead of Existing when you get to the screen in Figure 5-2. From there, follow these steps:

1. **Enter your first and last names on the screen.**

   Google asks you for your name in the screen shown in Figure 5-4. This is how they personalize any communications they have with you. Enter them and tap Next on the keypad.

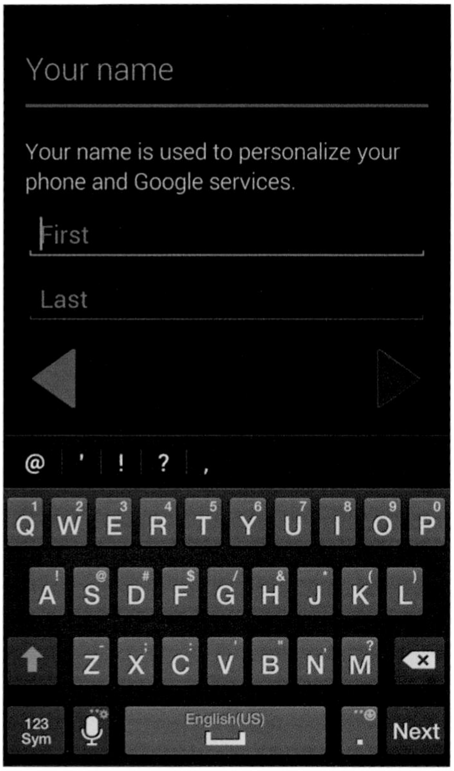

Figure 5-4: Enter your first and last name on this screen.

2. Enter the username you want to use with Gmail and tap Done.

On the screen shown in Figure 5-5, enter the username you want. Hopefully you get this name on the first shot.

If your first choice isn't available, try again. There is no easy way to check before you do these steps. Eventually, you hit on an unused ID. When you are successful, it will congratulate you.

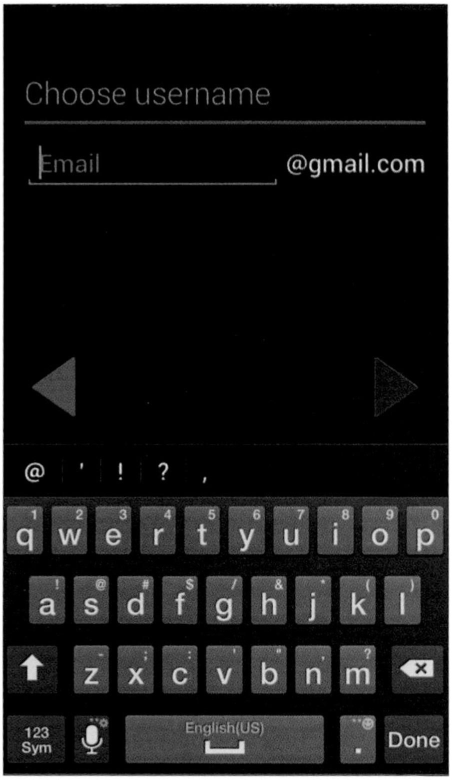

Figure 5-5: The Username screen.

3. Accept the terms and conditions of the account.

You may want a lawyer to review this. Or not. Basically, the terms are that you should be nice and not try to cheat anyone. Don't abuse the privilege of having the account.

4. Verify the funny-looking writing.

Google wants to make sure that you are a real person and not a computer program out to clog up a valid user ID. You will see a screen that looks like Figure 5-6.

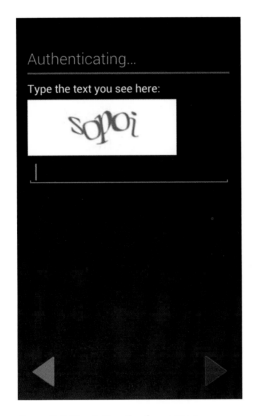

Figure 5-6: The Authenticating screen.

5. **Prepare a security question and an alternate e-mail address.**

If you forget your password, Google wants to verify that you are really you and not someone pretending to be you. They do this by asking you a security question and then asking for another e-mail account where they can send your temporary password. These screens in Figure 5-7 show you where to enter your information and the question choices.

6. **Join Google+ if you want.**

The next screen asks if you want to join Google+. You can if you want, but I suggest that you come back to it another time. The sooner you get your Gmail account set up, the more fun you can have. Tap Done.

After you tap Done, light flashes and you see the screen shown in Figure 5-8.

It usually takes less than five minutes. While you wait, you'll see all kinds of messages that it is getting ready to sync things. Don't worry. I'll explain these messages in good time. For now, you can add any other e-mail accounts you want by following the steps in the next section.

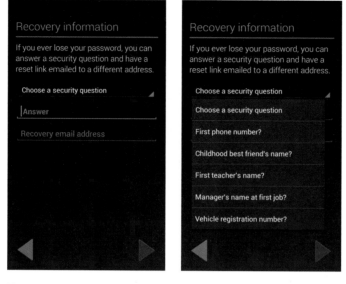

Figure 5-7: The Recovery Information screens.

Figure 5-8: The Waiting screen.

Working with non-Gmail e-mail accounts

Your phone is set up to work with up to ten e-mail accounts. If you have more than ten accounts, I'm thinking that you might have too much going on in your life. No phone, not even the Galaxy S 4, can help you there!

To set up an e-mail account other than Gmail to work with your phone, go to the Home screen. Look for the simple Mail icon; it has an envelope icon on it (see Figure 5-1). This is probably on your Home screen as one of the four primary shortcuts just above the Device Function keys or in your application list.

After you tell your phone all your emails, the first Email screen will have all your e-mails from all your e-mail accounts. This allows you to look at all the messages. In addition, each account has its own inbox. You can choose which option works best for you.

1. **Tap the Menu icon from the Email screen.**

   This brings up a menu that looks like the image shown in Figure 5-9.

2. **Tap the Others icon.**

   This is a generic way to enter lots of kinds of e-mail accounts. Tapping it brings up a screen that looks like the image shown in Figure 5-10.

3. **Carefully enter your full e-mail account name, and then enter your password in the second field.**

   Your e-mail address should include the full shebang, including the @ sign and everything that follows it. Make sure to enter your password correctly, being careful with capitalization if your e-mail server is case-sensitive — most are. If in doubt, select the option to let you see your password.

4. **Decide whether you want this account to be your default e-mail account.**

   After you add multiple accounts to your phone, only one account can be your primary, or default, account. Although you can send an e-mail from any of the accounts registered on your phone, you have to select one as the default. If you want this account to be the primary or default account, select the Send Email from This Account by Default check box. If not, leave that option as it is.

5. **Tap Next.**

   You see all kinds of options you can select. Just go with the default settings for now.

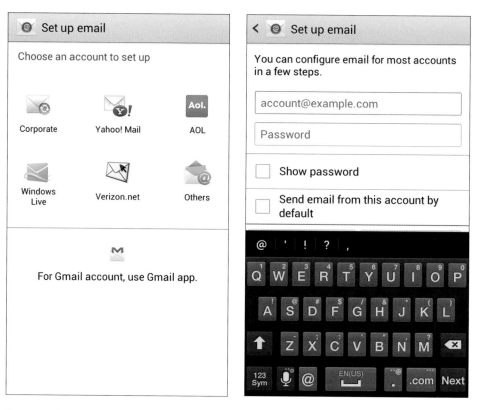

Figure 5-9: The menu for the Email app.   Figure 5-10: The Set Up Email screen.

6. **Tap OK.**

   If everything goes as planned, your phone and your e-mail account will start chatting.

7. **Enter names for the new e-mail account.**

   You can always use the e-mail address for the name, but I recommend choosing something shorter, like Joe's MSN or My Hotmail.

8. **Tap Done.**

Don't forget to check that everything has gone as planned and is set up to your liking. Go back to the Home screen, tap the Email icon, open Settings, and tap the + (plus) sign to add new accounts.

Using Figure 5-11 as an example, you can see that my account is now registered on my phone. It worked!

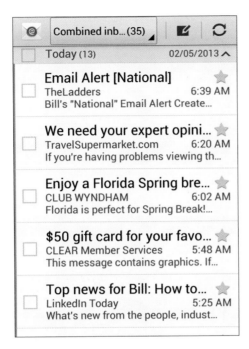

Figure 5-11: The Email Home screen.

Setting up a corporate e-mail account

In addition to personal e-mail accounts, you can add your work e-mail to your phone — if it's based upon a Microsoft Exchange server, that is, and if it's okay with your company's IT department.

Before you get started, you need some information from the IT department of your company:

- ✔ The domain name of the office e-mail server
- ✔ Your work e-mail password
- ✔ The name of your exchange server

If the folks in IT are okay with you using your phone to access its e-mail service, your IT department will have no trouble supplying you with this information.

Before you set up your work e-mail on your phone, make sure that you have permission. If you do this without the green light from your company, and you end up violating your company's rules, you could be in hot water. Increasing your productivity won't be much help if you're standing out in the parking lot holding all the contents of your office in a cardboard box.

Assuming that your company wants you to be more productive with no extra cost to the company, the process for adding your work e-mail starts at your e-mail Home screen seen in Figure 5-9. In fact, all the steps are the same as the previous section up to Step 4, so use those steps and then come back here in place of Step 5.

1. **Tap Manual Setup.**

   In Figure 5-12, I have closed the keypad and can see the full screen. Tap Manual Setup.

2. **Tap Exchange Account.**

   This brings up a screen like that shown in Figure 5-13. Some of the fields might be populated based upon the information that you entered at Step 5 in the preceding step list.

Figure 5-12: The full Set Up Email screen.

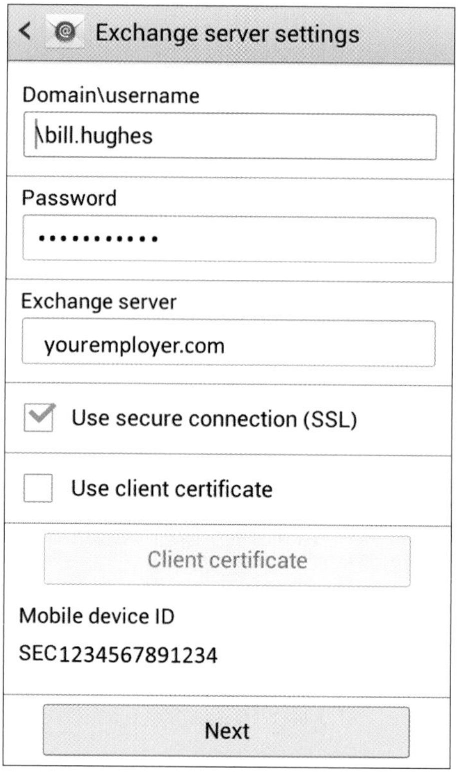

Figure 5-13: The Manual Setup screen for adding corporate e-mail accounts.

3. **Verify that information and enter any missing data according to what your IT department provided you.**

4. **Tap Next.**

   This begins synching with your work e-mail.

   Within a minute, you should start seeing your work e-mail messages appearing. If this doesn't happen, contact the IT department at your employer.

Reading E-Mail on Your Phone

In Figure 5-11, you can see how the e-mail screen looks for e-mail when you have multiple e-mail accounts. This screen is set up so that it combines all your e-mails into one inbox. At any given time, you might want to look at the accounts individually or all together.

To look at all your e-mails in one large inbox, tap Combined Inbox. This lists all your e-mails in chronological order. To open any e-mail, just tap it.

If, on the other hand, you want to see just e-mails from one account, tap the box at the top that says Combined Inbox. When you tap it, it displays a drop-down menu with all the individual e-mail accounts. Tap on the account you want to focus on at the moment, and your phone will bring up your e-mails in chronological order for just that e-mail address.

Writing and Sending an E-Mail

After you set up the receiving part of e-mail, the other important side is composing and sending e-mails. At any time when you're in an e-mail screen, simply tap the Menu button to get a pop-up screen.

There, tap the Compose icon shown in the following figure.

Here's the logic as to which e-mail account will be assigned to ultimately send this e-mail:

- ✓ If you're in the inbox of an e-mail account and you tap the Compose icon after tapping Menu, your phone sends the e-mail to the intended recipient(s) through that account.

- ✓ If you're in the combined inbox or some other part of the e-mail application, your phone assumes that you want to send the e-mail from the default e-mail account that you selected when you registered your second (or additional) e-mail account.

When you tap the Compose icon in the Menu pop-up menu, it tells you which account it will use. The Email composition screen in Figure 5-14 shows this e-mail will be coming from this account: `galaxysfordummies@gmail.com`.

Figure 5-14: The Email composition screen.

As shown in this screen, the top has a stalwart To field, where you type the address of the intended recipient. You can also call up your contacts, a group, or your most recent e-mail addresses. (Read all about contacts in Chapter 6.) You tap the address or contact you want, and it populates the To field.

Below that, in the Subject field, is where you enter the subject of the e-mail. And below that is the body of the e-mail, with the default signature, `Sent from my Samsung Galaxy S 4`, although this signature might have been customized for your cellular carrier.

At the top of the screen are two icons:

- ✔ **Send:** Tap this icon, which looks like an envelope with an arrow, to send the e-mail to the intended recipient(s).
- ✔ **Attach:** Tap this paperclip icon to attach a file of any variety to your e-mail.

If you change your mind about sending an e-mail, you can just tap the Back key. If you're partially done with the message, you're asked whether you want to save it in your Drafts folder.

The Drafts folder, seen in Figure 5-15, works like the Drafts folder in your computer's e-mail program. When you want to continue working on a saved e-mail, you open the Drafts folder, tap on it, and continue working.

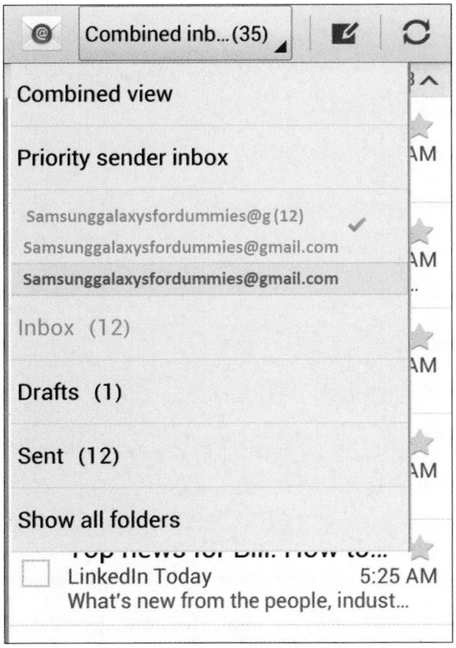

Figure 5-15: Email folders stored on your phone.

Replying to and Forwarding E-mails

Replying to or forwarding the e-mails that you get is a common activity. You can do this from your Email app. Figure 5-16 shows a typical open e-mail.

Figure 5-16: An opened e-mail.

You can Reply by tapping the button with the return arrow visible at the top of the screen. If other people were copied on the email, there will be a single return arrow to Reply to just the sender and a double return arrow you can tap to Reply All.

When you tap either of these options, the Reply screen comes back with the To line populated by the sender's e-mail address (or addresses) and a blank space where you can leave your comments.

To forward the e-mail, tap the appropriate Menu option of the Device Function keys. After you tap Forward, you enter the addressee just like you do when sending a new e-mail.

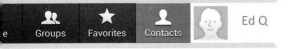

Managing Your Contacts

In This Chapter

▶ Putting all your callers, texters, and e-mailers on your phone

▶ Getting all your contacts in one location

▶ Keeping up to date with just a few taps

ou're probably familiar with using contact databases. Many cellphones automatically create one, or at least prompt you to create one. You also probably have a file of contacts on your work computer, comprising work e-mail addresses and telephone numbers. And if you have a personal e-mail account, you probably have a contact database of e-mail accounts of friends and family members. If you're kickin' it old school, you might even keep a paper address book with names, addresses, and telephone numbers.

The problem with having all these contact databases is that it's rarely ever as neat and tidy as I've just outlined. A friend might e-mail you at work, so you have her in both your contact databases. Then her e-mail address might change, and you update that information in your personal address book but not in your work one. Before long, you have duplicated contacts and out-of-date contacts, and it's hard to tell which is correct. How you include Facebook or LinkedIn messaging in your contact profile is unclear.

In addition to problems keeping all your contact databases current, it can be a hassle to migrate the database from your old phone. Some cellular carriers or firms have offered a service that converts your existing files to your new phone, but it's rarely a truly satisfying experience. You end up spending a lot of time correcting the assumptions it makes.

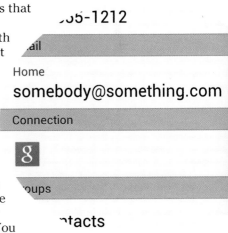

You now face that dilemma again with your Galaxy S 4: deciding how to manage your contacts. The purpose of this chapter is to give you the information on the advantages of each approach so that you can decide which one will work best for you. That way, you won't have the frustration of wishing you had done it another way before you put 500 of your best friends in the wrong filing system.

Bringing It All Together

Your phone wants you to have the ability to communicate with everyone you would ever want to in any way that you know how to talk to them. This is a tall order, and your Galaxy S 4 makes it as easy as possible. In fact, I would not be surprised if the technology implemented in the Contact application becomes one of your favorite capabilities in the phone. After all, your phone is there to simplify communication with friends, family, and co-workers, and the Contacts application on your phone makes it as easy as technology allows.

At the same time, this information is only as good as your contact database discipline. The focus of this chapter is to help you to help your phone to help you.

So far, you've seen how to make and receive calls, how to make and receive texts, and make and receive e-mails. You've started with an empty contact database. You may have noticed that you have been invited to make the calls and texts that you sent or received into contacts. In this chapter, I cover how to do that.

Using the Galaxy S 4 Contact Database

The fact of the matter is that if you introduced your phone to your e-mail accounts back in Chapter 5, the Contacts list on your phone has all the contacts from each of your contact lists.

Learning the Contact Database on your phone

Take a look at it and see. From your Home screen, tap the following icon.

If you have not created a Gmail account, synced your personal e-mail, or created a contact when you sent a text or made a call, your Contacts list will be empty. Otherwise, you will see a bunch of your contacts are now on your phone, sorted alphabetically like shown in Figure 6-1.

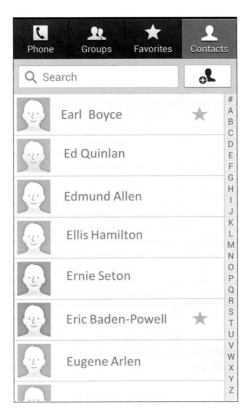

Figure 6-1: The Contacts list.

This database, and the Contacts application that manages the data, does more than just store names, phone numbers, and e-mail addresses. It can include the following information:

- The first and last name of the contact in separate fields
- All telephone numbers, including
    - Mobile
    - Home

- Work
- Work fax
- Pager
- Other

✔ E-mail addresses

- Home
- Work
- Mobile

✔ Up to nine IM addresses, including all the largest IM services (such as Google Talk, AIM, Windows Live, and Yahoo!)

✔ Company

✔ Job Title

✔ Nickname

✔ Mailing address for

- Home
- Work
- Another location

✔ Any notes about this person

- Web address
- Birthday
- Anniversary

Then, as if this weren't enough, you can assign a custom ringtone to play when this person contacts you. I cover the steps to assign a music file to an individual caller in Chapter 12.

Finally, you can assign a picture for the contact. It can be one out of your Gallery; you can take a new picture; or as I discuss in Chapter 8, you can connect a social network, like Facebook, which will then use that contact profile picture.

Fortunately, the only essential information is a name. Every other field is optional, and is only displayed if there is information to be displayed. See Figure 6-2 to see a sparsely populated contact.

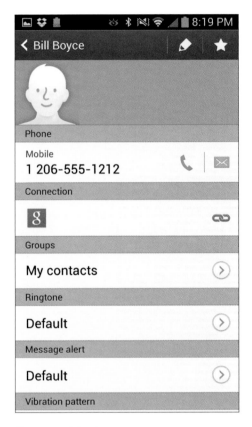

Figure 6-2: A basic contact.

This Contacts list is smart. Allow me to explain some of the things that are going on.

Say your best friend is Bill Boyce. You sent Bill a text earlier to let him know about your new phone. You followed the instructions in Chapter 4 and entered his telephone number. Without instruction, you took it to the next step and tapped Add Contact. You were prompted to add his name, which you did. Now your phone has a contact, "Bill Boyce."

Then you linked your e-mail. Of course your buddy Bill is in your e-mail Contacts list. So while you were reading this chapter, several things happened. First, your phone and your Gmail account synced. Your phone thinks about it, and figures this must be the same person. It automatically combines all the information in one entry on your phone!

Then your phone automatically updates your Gmail account. On the right side of Figure 6-3, you see the Google logo just beneath the e-mail address. That means that this contact is synced with the Gmail account. You did not have to do anything to make this happen.

Your phone noticed that Bill's work number was in your e-mail contact information, but the mobile phone number you used to text him was not. No problem! Now the contact on your phone includes both the information you had in your e-mail contact as well as his cellular phone.

Linking Contacts on your phone

Now, as slick as this system is, it isn't perfect. In this scenario, both contacts have the same first and last name. However, if the same person has a different name, you have to link these contacts. For example, if you created a contact for Bill Boyce, but your e-mail refers to him as William D. Boyce, your phone will assume that these are two different people.

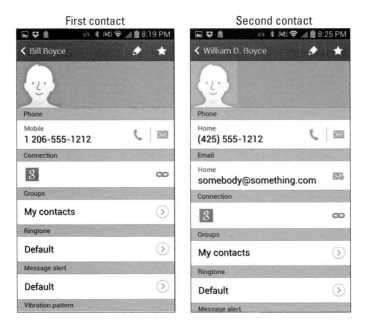

Figure 6-3: Two contacts for the same person.

No problem, though. Do you see the chain links icon in Figure 6-3 in the box that says Connection? Here are the steps to link the two contacts for the same person:

1. **From a contact, tap on the chain icon.**

   This brings up the pop-up shown in Figure 6-4.

   Choose the contact whose name you want to be the primary name. For example, I tapped the link on the William D. Boyce contact. That will be the name used on the combined contact going forward.

2. **Tap the Join another Contact button at the bottom of the screen.**

   Your phone will try to help you with some suggestions. This is seen in Figure 6-5. If it gets it all wrong, you can just find the other contact by searching alphabetically.

3. **Tap the Contact you want joined.**

   In this case, the second guess, Bill Boyce, is the one you want. Tap this name. The result is shown in Figure 6-6.

The combined link has all the information on this person.

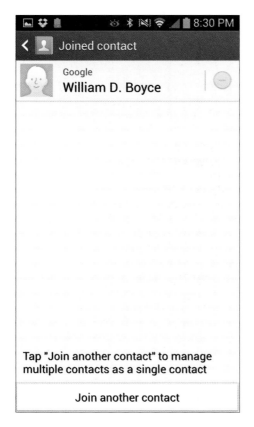

Figure 6-4: The linking page for William D. Boyce.

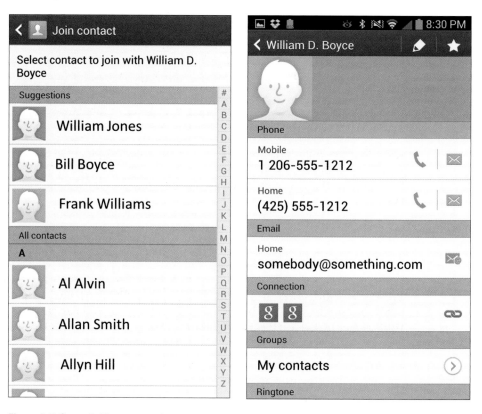

Figure 6-5: Some linking suggestions.

Figure 6-6: The linked contacts.

Grasping the link between the Contact database on your phone and Gmail

If you created a Gmail account back in Chapter 5, realize that your phone and this account automatically share all the contact information. This happens without you having to do anything. It just works. When you update your phone, the Gmail account automatically updates. When you update your Gmail account, your phone automatically updates.

In addition to being smart, here are some good reasons why you'd want to use your Gmail account to store your contact, rather than relying on a database stored solely on your phone:

✔ You don't lose your database if you lose your phone.

✔ If more of your social time is spent on your computer and you use your phone only occasionally, having the database on your computer be the most accurate is probably more valuable.

✔ As nice as the keyboard and screen are on the Galaxy S 4, it's easier to make additions, changes, and deletions to a database when you use a full keyboard and large screen. It's your choice.

Keep in mind that your phone stores a copy of all contacts in case you are unable to connect to your Gmail account, but the "official" copy of your contacts is stored away from your phone and safely hosted by your friends at Google.

Entering the Contacts on Your SIM Card

If your previous phone worked with AT&T or T-Mobile, you probably have a SIM card. Figure 6-7 shows a profile of a typical SIM card, next to a dime for scale, although yours probably has the logo of your cellular carrier nicely printed on the card. To the right of the SIM card is the newer micro SIM card. This is the same idea, but in a smaller package.

Figure 6-7: A SIM card and a micro SIM card.

If your cellular carrier was Verizon, Sprint, or US Cellular, you may be confused. Your Galaxy S 4 has a SIM card. What's the story? These carriers use CDMA technology for voice and some data. The phones using CDMA technology and data services up to 3G did not use a SIM card. Today, *all* carriers in the US are implementing a super high-speed data technology called LTE, also called 4G. Because your phone is capable of LTE, you now have a SIM card.

Like many users, you probably have stored your phone contacts on your SIM card. Some GSM-based phones allowed you to store your contacts on internal memory within the phone. This allowed you to store more contacts and more information on each contact than you could on the SIM card. However, in most cases, you probably stored your contacts on the SIM card. I suggest that you move them off and integrate them with your other contacts. Here is how to do this:

1. **From the Home screen, tap on Contacts.**

   You know how to do this.

2. **Tap the Menu key.**

   This brings up the pop-up screen in Figure 6-8.

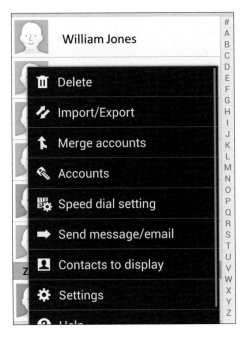

Figure 6-8: The Contacts menu pop-up screen.

These are all the options for Contacts.

3. **Tap the Import/Export option.**

   This brings up the screen in Figure 6-9.

4. **Tap Import from SIM Card.**

   It imports this information, and while you do other things, it syncs everything on your phone and then your Gmail account.

Figure 6-9: The Import/Export options.

Creating Contacts within Your Database

Your phone is out there trying to make your phone the ultimate contact database with as little effort on your part as possible. The interesting thing is that the salesperson in the cellular store did not really explain this to you. It is a subtle but important capability that is hard to communicate on the sales floor. Here is what happens.

Whenever you make or receive a call, send or receive an e-mail, or send or receive a text, your phone will look up that telephone number or e-mail address to check if it has seen it before. If it has, it will have all the other information on that person ready. If it does not recognize that telephone number or e-mail, it will ask if you want to make it a contact. What could be easier?

Adding contacts as you communicate

When you receive a call, a text, or an e-mail from someone who isn't in your Contacts list, you're given the option to create a profile for that person. The same is true when you initiate contact with someone who isn't in your Contacts list. Back in Chapter 3, you saw the dialing screens seen in Figure 6-10.

Figure 6-10: The dialing screens.

When you tap Add to Contacts, you're immediately given the option to create a contact or update an existing contact. Your phone doesn't know whether this is a new number for an existing contact or a totally new person. Rather than make an assumption (like lesser phones on the market would do), your phone asks you whether you need to create a new profile or add this to an existing profile.

Adding contacts when you are dialing

1. **Tap the Phone icon.**

   When you first bring up the Phone application, it brings up the keypad with a blank screen, as seen in the left screen in Figure 6-10.

2. **Start dialing the number**

   When you start entering the first number, you get a pop-up that asks if you want to Add to Contacts.

   Be patient. As you continue to type, your phone tries to guess whose name you are typing. Figure 6-11 sees that the digits you have typed are included in the phone number for your good buddy Robert Baden-Powell. As a courtesy, it tries to offer you the ability to save your tapping finger and just call Robert.

If Robert isn't the right one, you can see that there is another person with that number sequence in your Contacts list. If you mean to call the other person and not Robert, you can tap on the 2, and one of these contacts will be called.

However, if you're dialing a new number for the first time, just keep on typing. It will take those digits until it no longer recognizes the number. Eventually it gives up and shows you Figure 6-12.

Keep on typing until you have the complete number dialed.

3. When done typing, tap Add to Contacts.

4. Tap Save to Phone.

This brings up the option to save it as a new contact or to add this phone number to an existing contact.

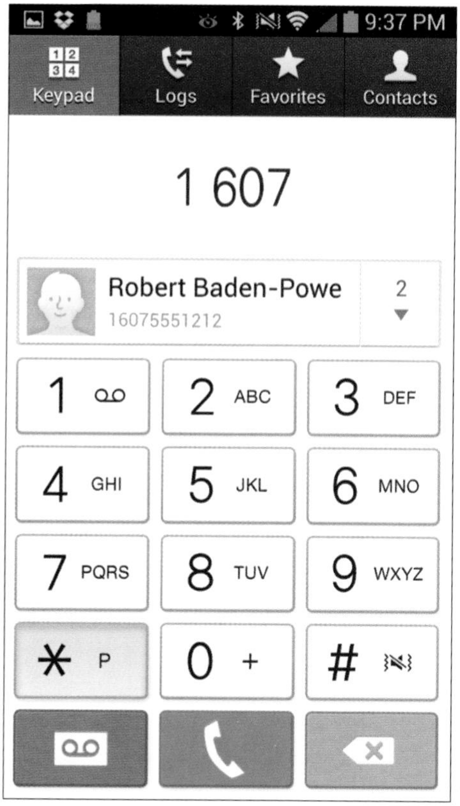

Figure 6-11: The Phone screen as you begin entering the phone number.

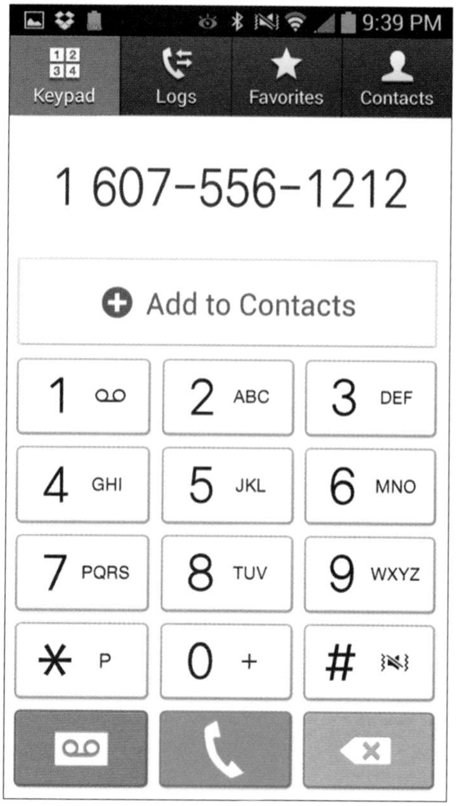

Figure 6-12: Eventually your phone gives up trying to guess an existing contact.

5. **Tap Create Contact.**

An empty contact profile like the one in Figure 6-13 appears.

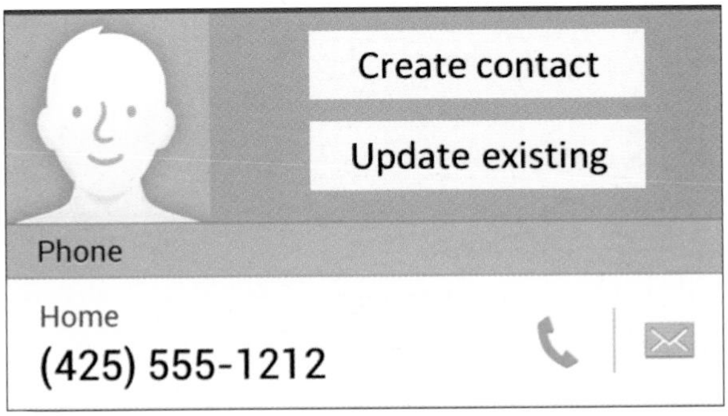

Figure 6-13: The Add to Contacts option.

Enter as much information on this contact as you want.

6. **Tap Save at the top of the screen.**

This contact will soon be synced with your Gmail account.

Adding contacts manually

Adding contacts manually involves taking an existing contact database and entering its entries to your phone, one profile at a time. (This option, a last resort, was the only option for phones back in the day.)

1. **Tap the Contacts icon.**

This brings up the screen shown in Figure 6-14.

2. **Tap the + (plus) sign.**

A screen with text boxes appears. This is the profile for the contact.

3. **Fill in the information that you want to include.**

This screen has defaults. For example, it assumes that you want to add the mobile phone number first. If you want to add the work or home number first, tap on Mobile to change the field description.

4. **If you want to add a second telephone number, tap the little green plus sign, and another text box shows up.**

5. **When you are done entering data, tap Save at the top of the screen.**

The profile is now on your phone. Repeat the process for as many profiles as you want to create.

Seeing How Contacts Make Life Easy

Phew. Heavy lifting over. After you populate the profiles of dozens or hundreds of contacts, you're rewarded with a great deal of convenience.

Start by tapping a contact. You see that person's profile, as shown in Figure 6-15.

All the options you have for contacting this contact are but a simple tap away:

- ✔ Tap the green telephone next to the number to dial that number.
- ✔ Tap the e-mail icon to create an e-mail.
- ✔ Tap the amber message balloon icon to send a text.

About the only thing that tapping on a data field won't do is print an envelope for you if you tap the mailing address!

Tap the plus sign.

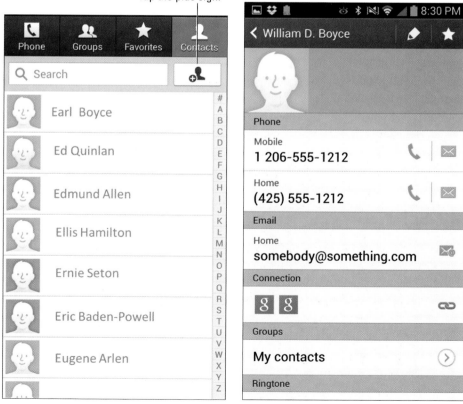

Figure 6-14: The Contacts List screen.　　　Figure 6-15: A basic contact profile.

Playing Favorites

Over the course of time, you probably find yourself calling some people more than others. It would be nice to not have to scroll through your entire contacts database to find those certain people. Contacts allows you to place some of your contacts into a Favorites list for easy access.

From within the Contacts app, open the profile and notice the star next to that person's name (refer to Figure 6-1). To the right of the contact name is a star. If that star is gold, that contact is a Favorite. If not, they're not.

To make them a star, tap on the blank outline of the star. To demote them from stardom but not delete them, tap on the gold star.

You won't immediately see a difference in your contacts other than the appearance of the gold star. When you open your Phone, however, this contact now appears under your Favorites tab. This is like a mini contact database. This is shown in Figure 6-16. It looks similar in structure to a regular contact database, but it includes only your favorites.

You can immediately find your Favorites from this tab and then dial that person by tapping his name and tapping Send.

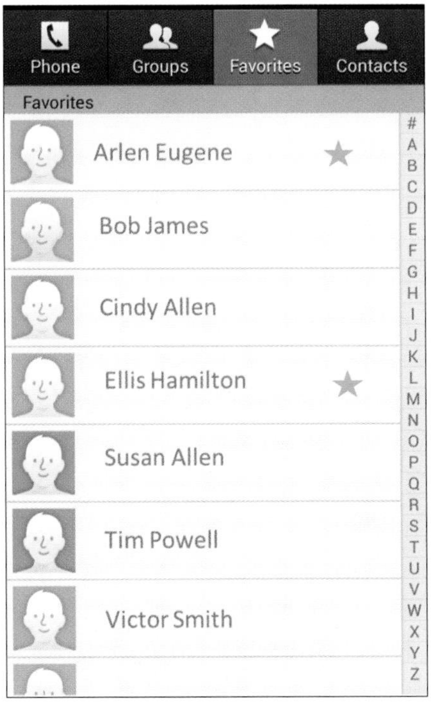

Figure 6-16: Contacts on the Favorites tab in Phone/Dialer.

Part III
Live on the Internet: Going Mobile

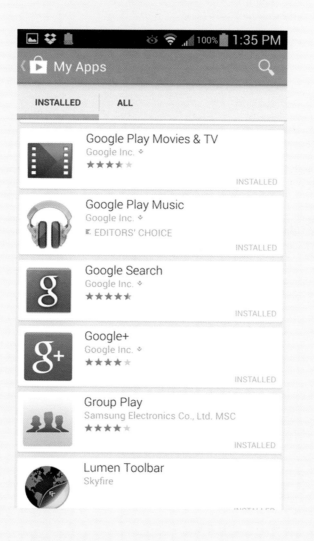

 Visit www.dummies.com/extras/samsunggalaxys4 for tips on how to buy books from the Play Store.

In this part . . .

- Surf the Internet from your phone and visit websites
- Get to know Google's Play Store and add exciting new apps to your phone
- Set the Browsing settings to quickly get to your favorite websites

You've Got the Whole (Web) World in Your Hands

In This Chapter

▶ Surfing the Internet from your phone

▶ Setting the Browsing settings for you

▶ Visiting websites

*1*f you're like most people, one of the reasons you got a smartphone is because you want Internet access on the go. You don't want to have to wait until you get back to your laptop or desktop to find the information you need online. You want to be able to access the Internet even when you're away from a Wi-Fi hotspot — and that's exactly what you can do with your Galaxy S 4 phone. In this chapter, I show you how.

The browser that comes standard with your Galaxy S 4 Phone works almost identically to the browser that's currently on your PC. You see many familiar toolbars, including the Favorites and search engine. And the mobile version of the browser includes tabs that allow you to open multiple Internet sessions simultaneously.

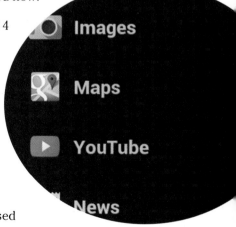

This chapter goes into much more detail on using the Internet browser on your Galaxy S 4 Phone as well as the websites that you can access from your phone.

For what it's worth, the browser on your phone is based upon Google's Chrome browser.

Starting the Browser

To launch the browser on your Galaxy S 4 phone, tap the Browser icon on one of the Home screens (shown in the following figure). Alternatively, tap the Application icon and then tap the Browser icon.

As long as you're connected to the Internet (that is, either near a Wi-Fi hotspot or in an area where you have cellular service), your home page appears. Your default home page could be blank or the Google home page, but most cellular carriers set their phones' home pages to their own websites or to a site selected by them.

If you're out of coverage range, or you turned off the cellular and Wi-Fi radios because you turned on Airplane mode, you'll get a pop-up screen letting you know that there is no Internet connection. (Read about Airplane mode in Chapter 2.)

If you should be in coverage but are not, or when you get off the airplane, you can reestablish your connections by pulling down the Notification screen and either tapping the Wi-Fi icon at the top or turning off Airplane mode.

Accessing Mobile (Or Not) Websites

After the browser is up, it's designed to function like the browser on your PC. At any time, you can enter a web address (the URL) by tapping the text box at the top of the screen.

For example, the page seen in Figure 7-1 is the mobile version of the website RefDesk.com.

You can get to this site by entering **m.refdesk.com** into the text block at the top from the software keyboard.

As a comparison, Figure 7-2 shows the PC version of this site. It has many more pictures, and the text is smaller. The mobile version loads faster, but looks less flashy.

RefDesk.com is far from the only website to offer a mobile version of its site. Many sites —from Facebook to Flickr, Gmail to Wikipedia — offer mobile versions.

So how do you get to the mobile version of your favorite websites? If a website has a mobile version, your phone browser will usually bring it up automatically. Samsung has gone out of its way to make the web experience on the Galaxy S 4 similar to what you experience when browsing the web on your desktop.

Figure 7-1: The mobile version of the website RefDesk.com.

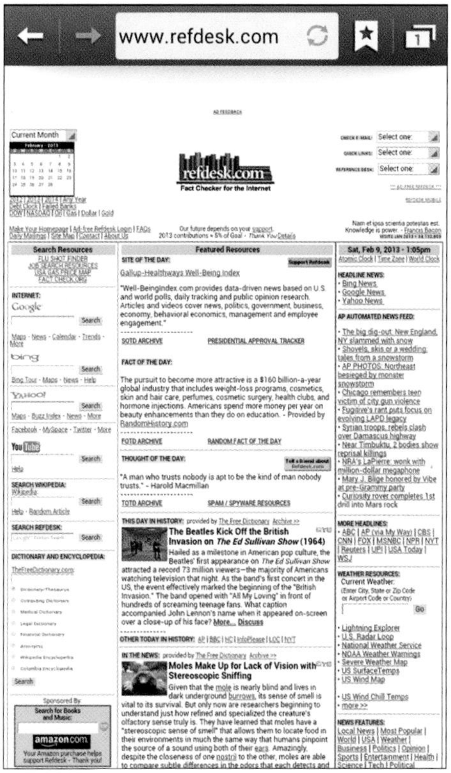

Figure 7-2: The PC version of RefDesk.com.

The most common differences between the address of a mobilized website and a regular one are

- **An m instead of www:** For example, the mobile version of `www.refdesk.com` is `m.refdesk.com`.

- **/mobile.com at the end of the address:** For example, the mobile version of Amazon.com is `www.amazon.com/mobile`.

If your phone doesn't automatically bring up the mobile version of a site, the simplest way to find it is to Google the desired site along with the term *mobile*. For example, the first option from Googling *Flickr mobile* on your phone is the mobilized website for Flickr.

When a site doesn't offer a mobile version (or when you just prefer to view the standard version of a particular site), you can stretch and pinch to find the information you need. (Stretch and pinch are hand movements you can use to enlarge/shrink what you see onscreen, as covered in Chapter 2.)

Navigating the Browser

With the browser active on your phone, as shown in Figure 7-3, the following are your options:

- **New Window:** Tap on the icon in the upper right corner with the 1 on the page. This brings up a screen, as seen in Figure 7-4.

  Here are your options:

  - If you just want a new window for a second browser section, tap the + (plus) sign. You get a second browser screen.

  - If you want to open a new window, but do it without your phone tracking what sites you've visited, tap the icon with a silhouette of a person in a trench coat and their hat pulled down. That brings up an incognito browser session. (Don't tell me why you want to do this. I don't need to know.)

  - If you just want to close an open window, you tap the red – (minus) sign next to the slightly smaller web page. It will disappear.

Tap for a new window.

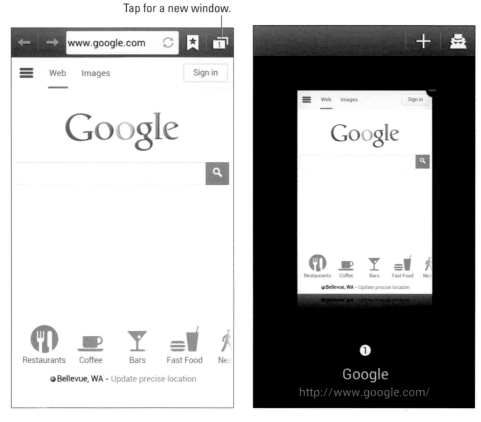

Figure 7-3: The open browser.

Figure 7-4: The New Window screen.

> ✓ **Bookmarks:** You can tap the icon seen in the following figure to make this site a favorite. I talk more about bookmarks in the next section.

✔ **Refresh:** Tap to resend data from the active tab. This is useful if there is no activity for a while. This is the same icon as on your desktop browser with the semi-circular arrows chasing each other's tails.

✔ **Back or Forward:** The Back and Forward buttons work just like the browser on your PC.

Using Bookmarks

As convenient as it is to type URLs or search terms with the keyboard, you'll find it's usually faster to store a web address that you visit frequently as a bookmark. Making bookmarks is a handy way to create a list of your favorite sites that you want to access over and over again.

The term *bookmarks* is roughly the equivalent of a Favorite on a Microsoft Internet Explorer browser.

In this section, I tell you how to bookmark a site and add it to your list of favorites. I also tell you how you can see your list of bookmarks.

Adding bookmarks

When you want to add a site to your bookmark list, simply visit the site. From there, follow these steps:

1. **Tap the Bookmark button.**

   This brings up a screen like that shown in Figure 7-5.

   Chance are that your carrier already put in a number of bookmarks. Some are for popular sites; others help you manage your account. The point is that you can add your own sites.

2. **Tap the button that says Add Bookmark.**

   This brings up a screen like Figure 7-6.

   The first textbox is the name you want to call it. In this case, the default is Mobile Refdesk. You can choose to shorten it to just Refdesk, or anything you want to call it. When ready, tap Next on the keyboard.

   The second textbox is the web address (URL). You probably want to leave this one alone. Just tap Next again.

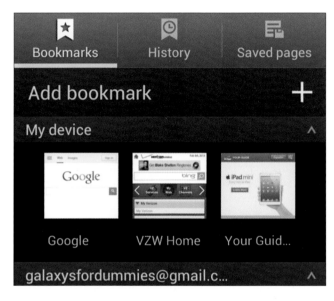

Figure 7-5: The Bookmarks screen.

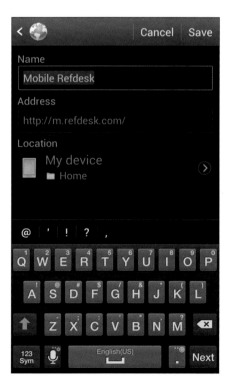

Figure 7-6: The Add Bookmark screen.

3. **Tap the Save button at the upper right corner of the screen.**

This puts a thumbnail of the website in your Bookmarks file. This is shown in Figure 7-7.

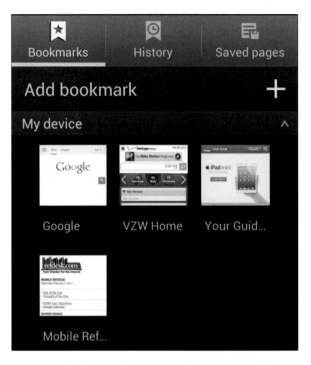

Figure 7-7: The Bookmarks screen with your new addition.

The next time you come to Bookmarks, you can tap this thumbnail, and this page will refresh and come up in its own window.

Bookmark housekeeping

Bookmarks are cool and convenient, but you don't always want to save them forever. Rather than have it take up prime real estate on your Bookmarks screen, you can delete it. Press and hold the thumbnail of the website you want to delete. This brings up a pop-up like in Figure 7-8.

To delete it, tap Delete Bookmark. It confirms that this is indeed what you want to do. Tap Yes and it's gone.

On the other hand, say you really like this site. You can make it your home page. Tap Set as Homepage. Boom. Done. It's your home page.

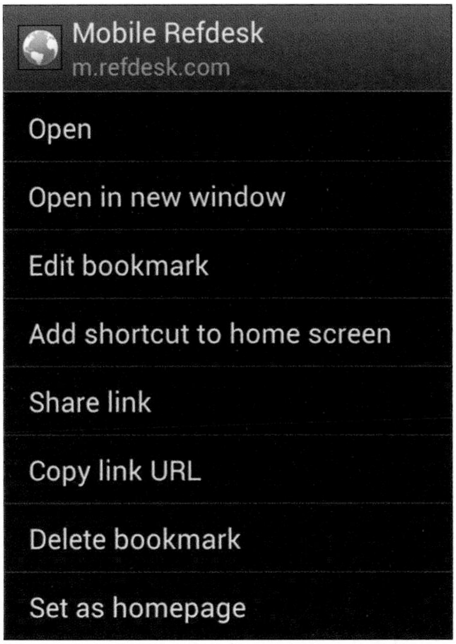

Mobile Refdesk
m.refdesk.com

Open

Open in new window

Edit bookmark

Add shortcut to home screen

Share link

Copy link URL

Delete bookmark

Set as homepage

Figure 7-8: Bookmark housekeeping options.

In addition to using bookmarks, you can also put a link on your phone's Home screen. This results in even faster access to your favorite websites.

To put a site on the Home screen of the phone, it must first be stored as a bookmark. From within the bookmark screen in Figure 7-8, tap Add Shortcut to Home Screen. When you return to the Home screen, you'll see an icon with the bookmark's name. When you want to see this web page, all you do is tap this icon, and a browser session opens with this as the web page.

Navigating Multiple Browser Sessions

As I mention earlier, it can be convenient to open multiple browser sessions — called _windows_ or _tabs_ — at the same time. Each window is open to its own website. You can jump around each session with ease without needing to load a new site each time. To jump among the windows, you tap the Tab Access icon. This is highlighted in Figure 7-9. As you can tell from the number on the Windows access button, there are three open windows.

1. **Tap the Windows access button.**

   This brings up a pop-up screen like that shown in Figure 7-10.

2. **Swipe to the page you want and Tap on it.**

   This brings the screen to full size.

   TIP

   The phone sometimes hides the icons for bookmarks and the Windows access button. If they are gone and you want them back, just press on the web page and slide your finger down. The icons reappear.

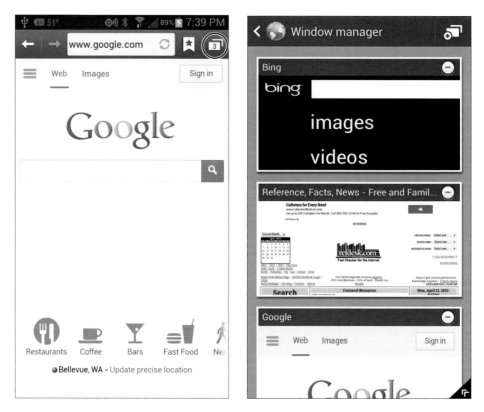

Figure 7-9: The screen for managing multiple browser sessions.

Figure 7-10: The housekeeping options for browser sessions.

Googling Your Way to the Information You Need: Mobile Google Searches

When you open the browser, you can use any search engine that you want (for example, Bing or Yahoo!). Still, some functions — web searches and map searches — work especially well when you use the Google search engine.

At the highest level, the search process works just like on your PC: You type (or tap) in a search topic, press Enter, and the search engine goes and finds it. Depending upon the search engine and your phone, you might even have the ability to speak your search topic aloud (searching by voice).

Android works well with the Google browser primarily because Android was developed by Google.

The Galaxy S 4 phone works to make Internet searches more convenient. Figure 7-11 shows the Google mobile web page.

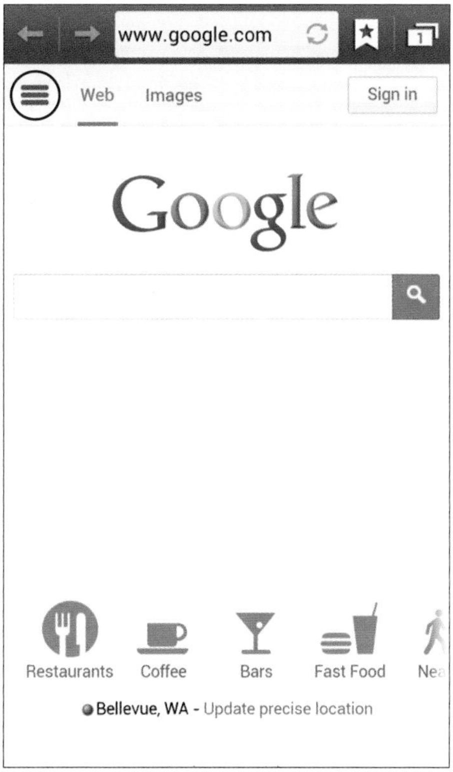

Figure 7-11: The Google mobile web page.

There are three nondescript bars off to the left that are circled in Figure 7-11. If you tap them, the screen slides to the right to expose Figure 7-12.

These searches are all available on Google, but clicking this button makes specific searches for images, videos, maps, and so on even easier to access.

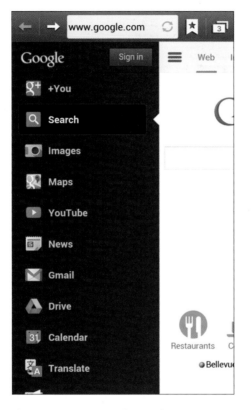

Figure 7-12: The secret Google Search icons.

8

Introducing Google's Play Store

In This Chapter

▶ Getting to know Play Store

▶ Finding Play Store on your phone

▶ Seeing what Play Store has to offer

▶ Downloading and installing Facebook for Android

▶ Rating and uninstalling apps

*O*ne of the things that makes smartphones (like the phones based upon the Google Android platform) different from regular cellphones is that you can download better applications than what comes standard on the phone. Most traditional cellphones come with a few simple games and basic applications. Smartphones usually come with better games and applications. For example, on your Galaxy S 4 phone, you get a more sophisticated contact manager, an application that can play digital music (MP3s), basic maps, and texting tools.

To boot, you can download even better applications and games for phones based on the Google Android platform. Many applications are available for your Galaxy S 4 Phone, and that number will only grow over time.

So, where do you get all these wonderful applications? The primary place to get Android apps is the Play Store. You might be happy with the applications that came with your phone, but look into the Play Store, and you'll find apps you suddenly won't be able to live without.

In this chapter, I introduce you to the Play Store and give you a taste of what you find there. For information on how to buy and download apps, keep reading.

Blurb Mobile Checkout
Blurb Inc.
★★★★☆

Manual updates

Chrome Browser - Google
Google Inc. ◇
★★★★☆

date

ShareCast Dongle

Exploring the Play Store: The Mall for Your Phone

The Play Store is set up and run by Google, primarily for the benefit of people with Android phones. Adding an application to your phone is similar to adding software to your PC. In both cases, a new application (or software) makes you more productive, adds to your convenience, and entertains you for hours on end — sometimes for free. Not a bad deal.

There are some important differences, however, between installing software on a PC and getting an application on a cellphone:

✔ **Smartphone applications need to be more stable than computer software because of their greater potential for harm.** If you buy an application for your PC and find that it's unstable (for example, it causes your PC to crash), sure, you'll be upset. If you were to acquire an unstable application for your phone, though, you could run up a huge phone bill or even take down the regional cellphone network. Can you hear me now?

✔ **There are multiple smartphone platforms.** These days, it's pretty safe to assume that computer software will run on a PC or a Mac or both. On the other hand, because of the various smartphone platforms out there, different versions within a given platform aren't always compatible. The Play Store ensures that the application you're buying will work with your version of phone.

Getting to the Store

You can access the Play Store through your Galaxy S 4 phone's Play Store application or through the Internet. I cover both of these methods in this section.

The easiest way to access the Play Store is through the Play Store application on your Galaxy S 4 phone. The icon is shown in the following figure.

If the Play Store application isn't already on your Home screen, you can find it in your Applications list. To open it, simply tap the icon.

When you tap the Play Store icon, you will be greeted by the screen shown in Figure 8-1.

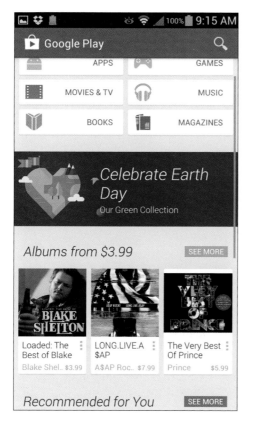

Figure 8-1: The Play Store home page.

As new applications become available, the highlighted applications will change, and the home page will change from one day to the next, but the categories will be consistent over time. These categories are

➞ **Apps:** This showcase highlights valuable applications or games that you might not otherwise come across. This is the first screen that you will see (the left-most screen on the panorama).

- ✔ **Games:** These apps are for fun and enjoyment. As it happens, these are the most-downloaded kind of applications. Popularity is a good initial indication that an application is worth considering.

    Throughout this book, I use the blanket term *applications* to refer to games and other kinds of applications. Some purists make a distinction between applications and games. The thing is, from the perspective of a phone user, they're the same. You download an application and use it, either for fun or to be more productive.

- ✔ **Music:** You can buy your digital music at the Play Store. I talk more about this in Chapter 12.

- ✔ **Books:** Have you been thinking about getting an e-reader, such as a Nook or a Kindle? Before you spend your hard-earned cash, take a look at the book library here and see if you like reading on your phone! If you like the way the Nook or the Kindle work, both are available as applications you can download and use to access your accounts on Barnes & Noble's website or Amazon.com.

- ✔ **Magazines:** Same idea as with books, only these are for periodicals.

- ✔ **Movies and TV:** As with music, you can download multimedia files and view your favorite movies and TV shows. You can watch these on your Galaxy S 4's screen or connect to your HD TV. More on this in Chapter 12.

Seeing What's Available: Shopping for Android Apps

When you head to the local mall with a credit card but without a plan, you're asking for trouble. Anything and everything that tickles your fancy is fair game. Similarly, before you head to the Play Store, it helps if you have a sense of what you're looking for, so you don't spend more than you intended.

The applications for your Galaxy S 4 phone fall into the following subcategories:

- ✔ **Games:** Your Galaxy S 4 phone takes interactive gaming to a new level. Games in this section of the Play Store fall into the following categories:

    - *Arcade and Action:* Think of games that are based upon arcades: shooting games, racing games, and other games of skill and/or strategy.

    - *Brain and Puzzle:* Think crossword puzzles, Sudoku, and other word or number games.

- *Cards and Casino:* Find an electronic version of virtually every card or casino game. (If you know of any game that's missing, let me know so I can write the application and sell it to the three people who play it.)

- *Casual:* This cross-over category includes simpler games, some of which are also arcade, action, or cards, but are distinguished by the ease with which you can pick it up and play and then put down. Solitaire may be the most widespread example of a casual game.

✔ **Applications:** The "non-games" fall into many subcategories:

- *Comics:* These are applications that are meant to be funny. Hopefully, you find something that tickles your funny bone.

- *Communication:* Yes, the Galaxy S 4 phone comes with many communications applications, but these Play Store apps enhance what comes with the phone: for example, tools that automatically send a message if you're running late to a meeting, or that text you if your kids leave a defined area.

- *Entertainment:* Not games per se, but these apps are still fun: trivia, horoscopes, and frivolous noise-making apps. (These also include Chuck Norris "facts." Did you know that Chuck Norris can divide by 0?)

- *Finance:* This is the place to find mobile banking applications and tools to make managing your personal finances easier.

- *Health:* This is a category for all applications related to mobile medical applications, including calorie counters, fitness tracking, and tools that help manage chronic conditions, such as diabetes.

- *Lifestyle:* This category is a catch-all for applications that involve recreation or specials interests, like philately or bird watching.

- *Maps & Search:* Many applications tell you where you are and where you want to go. Some are updated with current conditions, and others are based upon static maps that use typical travel times.

- *Multimedia:* The Galaxy S 4 phone comes with music and video services, but nothing says you have to like them. You might prefer offerings that are set up differently or have a selection of music that isn't available elsewhere.

- *News & Weather:* You find a variety of apps that allow you to drill down into getting just the news or weather that is more relevant to you than what's available on your extended Home screen.

- *Productivity:* These apps are for money management (like a tip calculator), voice recording (like a stand-alone voice recorder), and time management (for example, an electronic to-do list).

- *Reference:* These apps include a range of reference books, such as dictionaries and translation guides. Think of this as like the reference section of your local library and bookstore.

- *Shopping:* These applications help you with rapid access to mobile shopping sites or do automated comparison shopping.

- *Social:* These are the social networking sites. If you think that you know them all, check here. Of course, you'll find Facebook, LinkedIn, Twitter, Pinterest, and My Space, but there are dozens of other sites that are more narrowly focused that offer applications for the convenience of their users.

- *Sports:* Sports sites to tell you the latest scores and analysis can be found in this part of the Play Store.

- *Themes:* Your phone comes with color schemes or "themes." This part of the Play Store offers a broader selection.

- *Tools:* Some of these are widgets that help you with some fun capabilities. Others are more complicated, and help you get more functionality from your phone.

- *Travel:* These apps are useful for traveling, such as currency translations and travel guides.

- *Demo:* These are small, sometimes frivolous, applications that are in this catch-all category for those applications that don't quite fit anywhere else.

- *Software Libraries:* Computers of all sizes come with software libraries to take care of special functions, such as tools to manage ringtones, track application performance, and protect against malware.

Many of your favorite websites are now offering apps for your phone that are purposely built for your phone. I talked in the previous chapter about how you can access websites on your phone. You can use the full site with your high resolution screen or use the mobile version. A third alternative can be an app that makes it even easier to access the information you want from your phone.

Each application category comes with the applications divided into the following categories:

- ✔ **Top Paid:** All apps in this category have a charge.

- ✔ **Top Grossing:** These are the apps that are both popular and cost money. This is often a good indication that the app is really good, or at least that it has a crack marketing team. (If the app is not good, the customer comments will show that right away.)

- ✔ **Top Free:** None of the apps in this category have a charge.

- ✔ **Top Paid:** All apps in this category have a charge.

   ✔ **Trending:** Our friends at Google show the applications that are catching on. It is worth considering this category.

   ✔ **Featured:** These apps are relatively new, and might or might not have a charge.

In general, you'll probably want to see what you get with a free application before you spend money on it. Many software companies know this, and offer a lower-feature version for free and an enhanced version for a charge. Enjoy the free-market mechanisms on this site and never feel regret for enjoying a free application.

Installing and Managing the Facebook for Android App

To make this process less abstract, I'll show you how to download Facebook for Android as an example.

Downloading the Facebook app

When you want to add a site to your bookmark list, simply visit the site. From there, follow these steps:

1. **Open the Play Store.**

2. **In the Query box, type** Facebook.

   This brings up a drop-down screen like Figure 8-2.

3. **Tap on the line with the Facebook icon.**

   You want to get the Facebook *application*, so you can tap the line with the Facebook icon.

If you tap the line with the Facebook name, it brings up all the titles of apps, games, books, and magazines that include the Facebook name. This screen is seen in Figure 8-3.

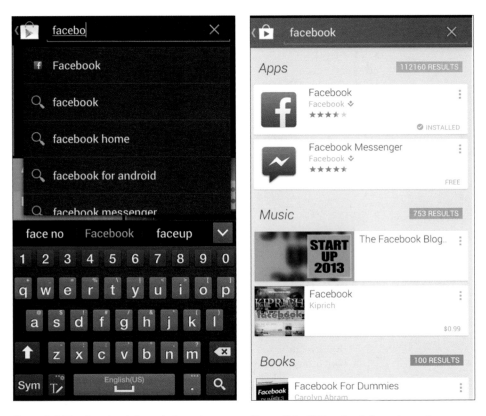

Figure 8-2: The Facebook Search drop-down menu.

Figure 8-3: All Facebook Search results.

As you can see in the search results, there are several options that include the word *Facebook*. The other lines in the apps section are for apps that include the word *Facebook*. These are typically for apps that "enhance" Facebook in their own ways. As of this moment, there are 112,160 of these. Rather than going through these one by one, stick with the one with the Facebook icon.

When you tap the Facebook app, you get a lot of information, as shown in Figure 8-4.

Figure 8-4: The Facebook app screen in panorama.

Before you continue to the next step, I want to point out some important elements on this page.

- **Title Line:** The top section has the formal name of the application with an Install button. After you click this to download and install the app, you'll see some other options. I give some examples later in this chapter.

- **Screen Captures:** These are representative screens. They are a little too small to read, but they do add some nice color to the page.

- **Feedback Statistics:** This particular app has about 3.5 stars out of five. That's not bad, but not great. The other numbers tell you how many folks have voted, how many have downloaded this app, the date it was released, and the size of the app in MB.

- **Rate and Review:** This is blank until you have downloaded the app that you would be voting on.

- **What's New:** This information is important if you have a previous version of this app. Skip this section for now.

- **Description:** This tells you what the app does.

- **Reviews:** This section gets into more details about what people thought beyond the star ranking.

- **More by Facebook:** The app developer in this case is Facebook. If you like the style of a particular developer, this section tells you what other apps they offer.

- **Users Also Installed:** Play Store tells you the names of other apps that the customers that downloaded this app. It is a good indicator of what else you may like.

- **Users Also Viewed:** Same idea as the previous bullet, but it's somewhat less of an endorsement. The other users only viewed these other apps. They didn't necessarily purchase them.

- **Developer:** This section gives you contact information on the developer of this app.

- **Google Play Content:** This is how you tell the Play Store whether this app is naughty or nice.

4. **Tap the button that says Install.**

Before the download process begins, the Google Play store tells you what this application plans to do on your phone. This screen is shown in Figure 8-5.

This information lists all the permissions you will be granting the application when you download it.

This is similar to the license agreements that you sign. Hopefully you read them all in detail and understand all the implications. In practice, you hope that it is not a problem if lots of other people have accepted these conditions. In the case of a well-known application like Facebook, you are probably safe, but you should be careful with less popular apps.

Back in Chapter 1, you were presented with the option to prevent an app from having access to your location information. I mentioned that you could allow apps to know where you are on a case-by-case basis. Here is where that issue comes up. Each app asks you for permission to access information, such as your location. If you do not want the app to use that information or share it somehow, here is where you would find out if the app uses this information. You may be able to limit the amount of location information. If you are not comfortable with that, you should decline the app in its entirety.

5. **Tap the Accept button.**

Before the download process starts, your app may want to know two things. First, do you want your phone to automatically update when Facebook (or the app provider) releases a newer version? In general, this is the most convenient option. It is rare, but not unheard of that an update makes things worse.

The second is whether you want to wait for the update to take place only when you have a Wi-Fi connection. This prevents your phone from downloading a huge application update over the cellular network. In most cases, using a Wi-Fi connection is a better option. Facebook asks you this question in the pop-up seen in Figure 8-6.

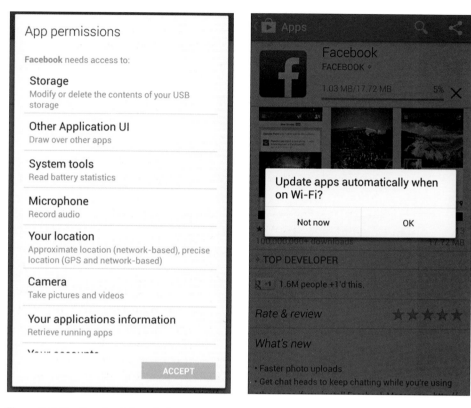

Figure 8-5: The Facebook Permissions screen.   Figure 8-6: The automatic update pop-up screen.

6. Tap OK.

This is like downloading apps to your PC over the Internet. The screens in Figure 8-7 show you the progress of downloading and installing the application.

This may happen so fast that you look away for a second and when you look back, it's done. Sometimes the Play Store offers you the option to keep on shopping while the app downloads in the background. If you like, you can watch the process in the notification portion of your screen.

Download   Installation

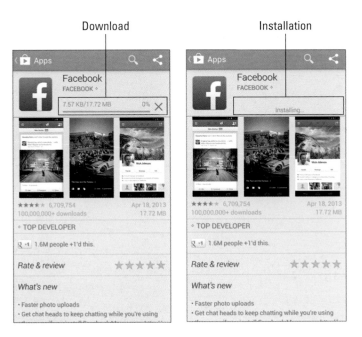

Figure 8-7: The Facebook download and installation screens.

Depending upon the speed of your connection, you will see a screen like Figure 8-8.

Apps immediately give you the option to either open them or uninstall.

The Facebook icon is now on your Apps screen along with some other recently added applications, like Angry Birds and Pandora in Figure 8-9.

If you want this app to be on your Home screen, press and hold the icon.

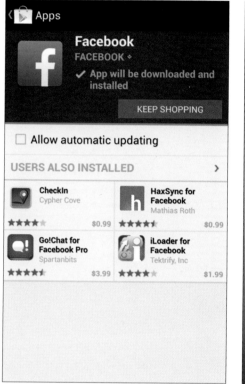

Figure 8-8: The Facebook app screen.

Figure 8-9: The Facebook icon on the Apps screen.

Creating an account

You can start immediately by tapping on Open from the Facebook App screen. You could also tap the Facebook icon from the Apps screen. If you added this app to your Home screen, you can tap its icon there. In any case, opening the app brings up the screen in Figure 8-10.

If you do not already have a Facebook account, you can create an account here. Towards the bottom of the screen is the option to sign up for Facebook.

If you already have a Facebook account, all you need to do is enter your e-mail address or phone number and Facebook password in the screen shown in Figure 8-10. Hopefully you can recall your Facebook password. It could be the same as your e-mail password, even though using the same password for multiple accounts is bad security discipline. Obviously, you will need to get back to your PC to figure it out if you cannot remember it.

To sign up for Facebook, use an e-mail account or your mobile number as well as a password. The first step is to enter your information on the screen shown in Figure 8-11.

After you enter this information, Facebook sends a verification message. If you provide an e-mail address, the app sends you an e-mail. If you use your mobile phone number, it sends you a text.

The e-mail or text contains a code. Enter this code, and your Facebook account is validated. To get the most out of Facebook, I recommend *Facebook For Dummies,* 4th Edition by Carolyn Abram.

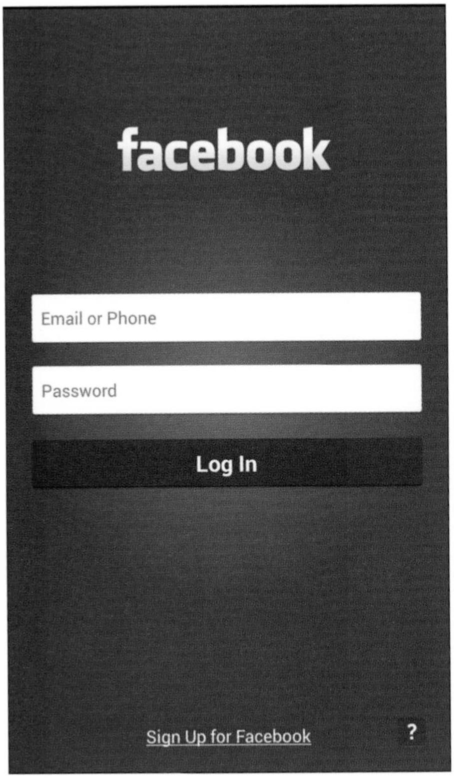

Figure 8-10: The Facebook Home screen.

Figure 8-11: The Sign Up for Facebook screen.

It will ask you questions about your preferences for syncing Contacts. You can choose to put all your Facebook friends in your phone's Contacts database. This goes so far as to use your Facebook image as your Contacts image. The options for syncing are seen in Figure 8-12.

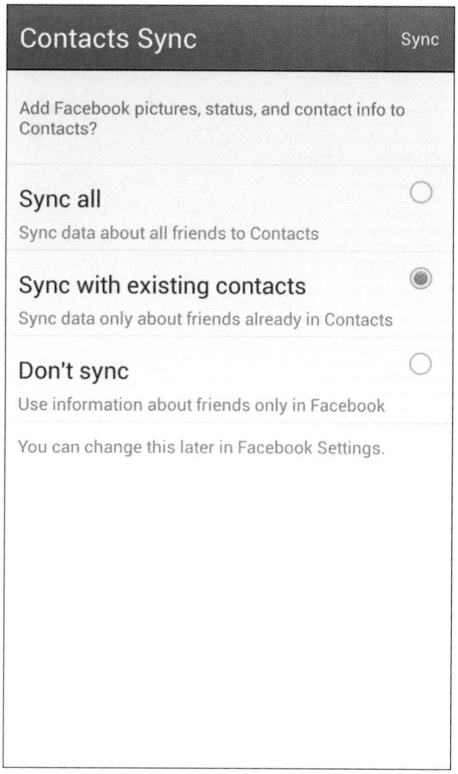

Figure 8-12: The Facebook Sync options.

- ✔ **Sync All:** This syncs with your existing contacts and makes new contacts for Facebook friends that do not already have an entry in your Contacts database.

- ✔ **Sync with Existing Contacts:** Same idea as the previous bullet, but if they do not already have an entry, it doesn't create a new contact.

- ✔ **Don't Sync:** As the name implies, this keeps Contacts as Contacts and Facebook friends as Facebook friends, and does not mix the two.

When you have made your selection, tap the word Sync, and it's done. It is really amazing all the ways that this information integrates into your phone. Pictures of your contacts start appearing in your Contacts database. You will see the option to post pictures from your Gallery to your Facebook Page, to name a few.

Within the Facebook app itself, you see the latest posts from your friends in an instant. You get your daily serving of cute kitten images, stories from proud parents about their children, and messages from old flames wondering about what might have been.

Managing Facebook Settings

You can get to the Facebook Settings by tapping on the Menu button and tapping settings. I urge you to consider how much you want to control how many of these capabilities you want continuously. Even the most hard-core Facebook fan may need a break from all the notifications.

Figure 8-13 shows you the options you have for settings. You can just go along with the defaults.

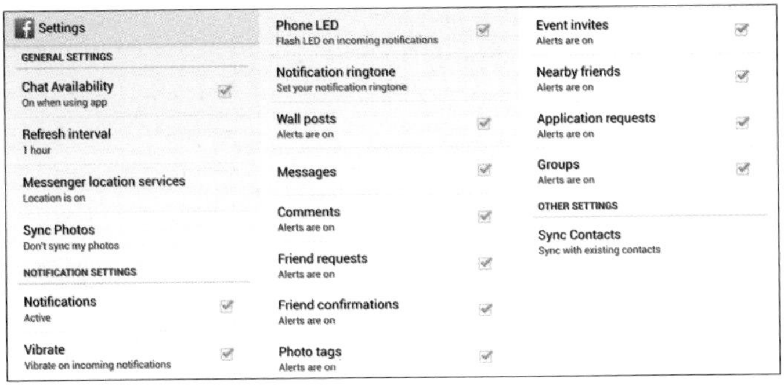

Figure 8-13: The Facebook Settings options.

Or if you prefer, you can also set it up to your liking. The options are

- **Chat Availability:** You can choose to chat or not when you are running this app.

- **Refresh Interval:** You get to decide how often the Facebook app polls the Internet to see if there are new posts. The default is every hour. Polling more often keeps you better informed, but it can drive up costs. Your choices are shown in Figure 8-14.

  If you choose Never, it looks for status updates only when you first open the app.

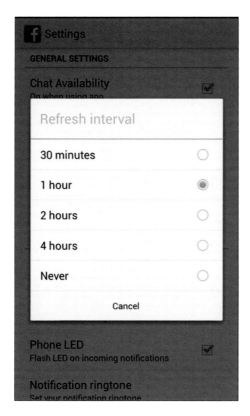

Figure 8-14: The Facebook Refresh Interval.

⮐ **Messenger Location Services:** If you change your mind about having Facebook know where you are, here is how you would change the setting.

⮐ **Sync Photos:** This option lets you share the images in your Gallery application with Facebook. This is a fun capability, but more than a few people have accidentally posted too many pictures from their phone to their Facebook page. My advice is to be sure that the photo you select in Gallery should be shared.

⮐ **Notifications:** The next bunch of options can all be turned off if you deselect the Notification check box. If you want some but not all of these notifications, leave the Notification check box selected, and deselect the notifications you do not want.

The next selections offer you methods on how you would be notified of a change on your Facebook.

• *Vibrate:* Every time something happens on Facebook, your phone vibrates.

+ *Phone LED:* Every time something happens on Facebook, an LED lights up.

+ *Notification Ringtone:* Every time something happens on Facebook, your phone makes a noise. Tap this line and you see all the options.

These selections let you select what Facebook events trigger a notification alert.

+ *Wall Posts*

+ *Messages*

+ *Comments*

+ *Friends Requests*

+ *Friend Confirmations*

+ *Photo Tags*

+ *Event Invites*

+ *Nearby Friends*

+ *Application Requests*

+ *Groups*

✔ **Sync Contacts:** This option brings back the screen from Figure 8-12 in case you want to change your Sync status.

There are lots of combinations and permutations for Facebook. Choose wisely.

Rating and Uninstalling Your Apps

Providing feedback to an application is an important part of the maintaining the strength of the Android community. It's your responsibility to honestly rate applications. (Or you can blow it off and just take advantage of the work others have put into the rating system. It's your choice.)

If you want to make your voice heard about an application, here are the steps:

1. **Open the Play Store.**

    See Figure 8-1.

2. **Tap the Menu button.**

    This brings up a drop-down menu like the one shown in Figure 8-15.

3. **Tap the Line that says My Apps.**

    This brings up the screen, shown in Figure 8-16, of a listing of all the apps that are on your phone. Keep scrolling down. You will eventually see them all.

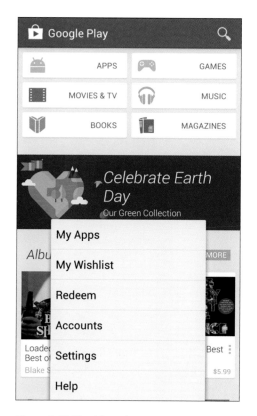

Figure 8-15: The Menu button drop-down menu from the Play Store.

Figure 8-16: The My Apps screen in panorama.

Tap on one of these apps to rate or uninstall it, as shown in Figure 8-17.

If you love the app, rate it highly. You get a pop-up, as shown in Figure 8-18, to rank it and tell the world what you think.

If you hate the app, give them one star and blast away. Then you can remove it from your phone by tapping the Uninstall button.

Uninstall option

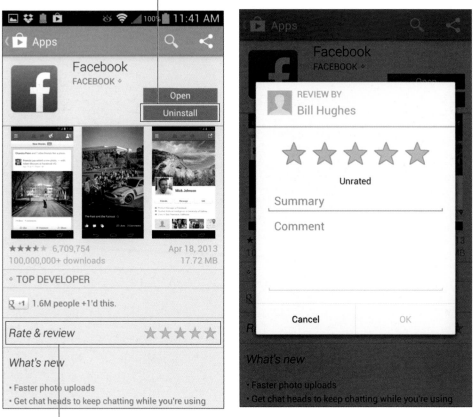

Figure 8-17: The My Apps page for Facebook.

Rate and Review

Figure 8-18: The Rating pop-up.

Part IV

Entertainment Applications

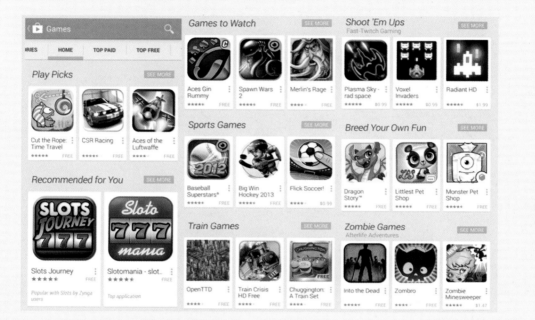

Visit www.dummies.com/extras/samsunggalaxys4 for tips on listening to Pandora Internet radio on your phone.

In this part . . .

- ✔ Taking pictures and video on your phone
- ✔ Perusing the games available on the Play Store and download-
  ing the best ones to your phone
- ✔ Keeping track of what you've downloaded
- ✔ Enjoying a single song, podcasts, or an entire album
- ✔ Knowing your licensing options

9

Sharing Pictures

In This Chapter

▶ Taking pictures and video on your phone

▶ Organizing your pictures and video

▶ Sharing pictures and video with friends and family

1 f you're like many cellphone users, you love that you can shoot photographs and video with your phone. You probably carry your phone with you practically everywhere you go, so you never again have to miss a great photograph because you left your camera at home.

And don't think that Samsung skimped on the camera on your Galaxy S 4. Boasting 13MP of muscle, this camera is complemented with lots of shooting options. Then, you can view your shots on that wicked Super AMOLED screen. Samsung also includes a Gallery app for organizing and sharing. Plus, the camera can shoot stills *and* video.

Stick with this chapter to see how to take a photograph, organize your photos, and share them with friends and family.

A super-fast primer on Super AMOLED

All Samsung Galaxy S 4 phones have a Super AMOLED screen. Allow me to take a moment to explain what makes this so good — and what makes you so smart for having bought this Samsung Galaxy S 4 phone.

To start, think about a typical LCD screen, like what your TV or PC might have. LCDs are great, but they work best indoors where it's not too bright. LCDs need a backlight (fluorescent, commonly), and the backlight draws a fair amount of power, although much less power than a CRT. When used on a phone, an LCD screen is the largest single user of battery life, using more power than the radios or the processor. Also, because of the backlight on an LCD screen, these screens display black as kinda washed-out, not a true black.

The next step has been to use light emitting diodes (LEDs), which convert energy to light more efficiently. Monochrome LEDs have been used for decades. They are also used in the mongo-screens in sports arenas. Until recently, getting the colors right was a struggle. (Blue was a big problem.) That problem was solved by using organic materials (*organic* as in carbon-based, as opposed to being grown with no pesticides) for LEDs.

The first organic LEDs (OLEDs) looked good, drew less power, and offered really dark blacks — but still had two problems. They really stunk in bright light, even worse than did LCD screens. Also there was a problem with *crosstalk*, where the individual pixels would get confused over time whether they were to be on or off. You would see green or red pixels remain, even if it the area around it was clearly supposed to be dark. It was very distracting.

The solution to the pixel's confusion is called Active Matrix, which tells the pixels more frequently whether they are to be on or off. When you have Active Matrix technology, you have an Active Matrix Organic LED, or AMOLED. This technology still stinks in bright light, however.

Enter the Super AMOLED technology, made by Samsung. When compared with the first AMOLED screens, Super AMOLED screens are 20 percent brighter, use 20 percent less power, and cut sunlight reflection by 80 percent. This is really super!

This screen still uses a significant share of battery life, but less than with earlier technologies. With Super AMOLED, you even save more power if you use darker backgrounds where possible.

Say Cheese! Taking a Picture with Your Phone

Before you can take a picture, you have to open the Camera app. The easiest way is to simply access the Camera application from the Application list. Just tap the Camera icon to launch the app.

A closely related application on your phone is the Gallery, which is where your phone stores your images. The icons for these two apps are shown in the following figure.

With the Camera app open, you're ready to take a picture within a few seconds. The screen becomes your viewfinder. You'll see a screen like the one shown in Figure 9-1.

Figure 9-1: The screen is the viewfinder for the Camera app.

And how do you snap the picture? Just tap the big Camera icon on the right: the camera within the oval. The image that's in your viewfinder turns into a digital image that you can set to either JPG or PNG format.

After you take a picture, you have a choice. The image is automatically stored in another application: Gallery. This allows you to keep on snapping away and come back to the Gallery when you have time. I cover the Gallery application more in the upcoming section, "Managing Your Photo Images."

For skeptics only

If you've ever used a cameraphone, you might be thinking, "Why make such a big deal about this camera's phone? Cameraphones aren't worth the megapixels they're made of." Granted, in the past, many cameraphones weren't quite as good as a digital camera, but Samsung has addressed these issues with the Galaxy S 4.

✔ **Resolution:** The resolution on most cameraphones is lower than what you typically get on a dedicated digital camera. The Galaxy S 4, however, sports an 8 megapixel (MP) camera — and that's good enough to produce a 5×7 inch print that's indistinguishable from what you could produce with an analog camera.

✔ **Photo transfer:** With most cameraphones, the photos are hard to move from the camera to a computer. With the Samsung Galaxy S 4, however (remember: it uses the Android operating system), you can quickly and easily send an image, or a bunch of images, anywhere you want, easily and wirelessly.

✔ **Screen resolution:** In practice, many cameraphone users just end up showing their pictures to friends right on their phones. Many cameraphone screens, however, don't have very good resolution, which means your images don't look so hot when you want to show them off to your friends. The good news is the Samsung Galaxy S 4 has a bright, high-resolution screen. Photos look really good on the Super AMOLED technology screen.

✔ **Organization:** Most cameraphones don't offer much in the way of organization tools. Your images are all just there on your phone, without any structure. But the Samsung Galaxy S 4 has the Gallery application that makes organizing your photos easier. It is also set up to share these photos easily.

However, if you want to send that image right away, here's what you do:

1. **From the viewfinder screen, tap the Last Image icon.**

   The viewfinder shows a thumbnail of the most recent image you took. This image is at the bottom right corner of the viewfinder. When you tap it, it brings up the Gallery application. This is seen in Figure 9-2.

   This brings up the current image along with the four most recent photos. It also brings up some options. Right now, you're interested in the highlighted Sharing button.

The Share button

Figure 9-2: The Gallery app.

2. **Tap the Share button.**

   This brings up the options you can use to forward the image; see Figure 9-3. These options include any of the following (although your phone might not support all the options listed here).

   - *Messaging:* Attach the image to a text message to someone's phone as an MMS message.

   - *Picasa:* Picasa is a website owned by Google, created to help its subscribers organize and share photos. The main advantage for subscribers is that they can send links to friends or family for them to see a thumbnail of images, rather than sending a large number of high resolution files. Read more on Picasa in the next section.

   - *Email:* Send the image as an attachment with your primary e-mail account.

   - *Bluetooth:* Send images to devices, such as a laptop or phone, linked with a Bluetooth connection.

   - *Group Play:* This is an application that allows you to share with DLNA and Wi-Fi devices.

     DLNA (Digital Living Network Alliance) is a trade group of several consumer electronics firms to create an in-home network among compatible devices. The goal is to make it easier to share music, videos, and photos. Your Galaxy S 4 is DLNA-compliant. If you have other DLNA devices, such as a TV, you can easily share your photos by using the AllShare app.

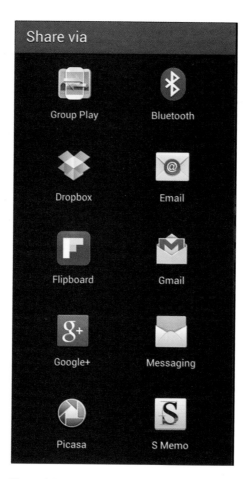

Figure 9-3: Sharing options for the current image.

- *Gmail:* If your main e-mail is with Gmail, this option and the Email option are the same.

- *Facebook:* In Chapter 8, I cover how to connect your phone with Facebook. You can take a picture and post it on your Facebook account with this option. This option appears as an option only after you download the Facebook app and register.

- *Wi-Fi Direct:* Talk about slick! This option turns your phone into a Wi-Fi access point so that your Wi-Fi–enabled PC or another smartphone can establish a connection with you.

- *Dropbox:* Dropbox is the same service that was offered when you first turned on your phone. It's in the *cloud* that everyone is talking about. It works like a hard drive or memory card as far as other apps are concerned, but it's really data storage space on the Internet. A limited amount of space is free for the taking. If you want more space, you can pay a monthly fee.

- *Flipboard:* This is another service that comes as an app pre-installed on your Galaxy S 4. It aggregates your different social networks.

- *S-Memo:* I cover this in Chapter 15 along with S-Voice.

> Of course, an account with Gmail (that is, an e-mail address that ends in @gmail.com) is entirely optional. However, there are advantages to having a Gmail account with your Android-based Galaxy S 4 phone: for example, you automatically become a subscriber to Picasa and other Google-owned services.

When you select one of these options, the image is automatically attached or uploaded, depending upon the nature of the service you selected. If one of these options doesn't suit your needs to share your pictures, perhaps you're being too picky!

Getting a Little Fancier with Your Camera

Using the default Camera settings to snap pics is perfectly fine for those candid, casual, on-the-go shots: say, friends in your well-lit living room. However, your Samsung Galaxy S 4 phone camera can support much more sophisticated shots. Your digital SLR camera has a bigger lens than your phone, but I can assure you that you phone has a much bigger brain than your camera. I cover the main options here, but if you want to get a lot fancier, play around with the settings to your heart's content.

The Mode setting

The Mode setting is where you make some basic settings that describe the situation under which you will be taking your shot. The default is a single picture in Automatic mode. The Mode icon is a round button underneath the button for the shutter release. Tapping on this icon brings up the options in Figure 9-4.

The options rotate as you flick through them. To have the options display in Panorama mode, as seen in Figure 9-5, tap the button with the four squares in the lower-left corner.

Tap to view Mode options in Panorama mode.

Figure 9-4: The Mode options on the camera viewfinder.

Figure 9-5: The Mode icons on the camera viewfinder.

Tapping the Mode icon brings up a number of choices:

- **Auto:** Taking a single photo at a time is the default setting, which assume average light. It's a good place to start.

- **Beauty Face:** This mode automatically hides subtle facial imperfections. (No guarantees!)

- **Best Photo:** This setting takes a quick series of three images per second for each press on the Camera icon; that way, you can later pick which one you really want. This option uses the same amount of memory and battery as taking six shots, which isn't much. And it makes it more likely that everyone's eyes will be open!

✔ **Best Face:** This is a combination of the previous two.

✔ **Sound & Shot:** This option records the ambient sound when you take a photo. This adds dimension to the still image.

✔ **Drama:** The thumbnail image of the snowboarder in Figure 9-5 shows what you can do with this option. The background does not move, but you get multiple shots of the person in motion.

✔ **Animated Photo:** This option allows you to blend a still shot with a moving image. This is for the really creative among us.

✔ **Rich Tone (HDR):** Rich Tone mode automatically enhances the depth of the colors in your shot.

✔ **Eraser:** Have you ever been taking a picture when a clueless pedestrian unexpectedly walks into the viewfinder just as you snap? You want to take that fool out. Now you can (digitally remove them from the shot, that is). The camera takes a few extra images so you can see what was blocked, and your phone recreates the image without the pedestrian.

✔ **Panorama:** Take a wider shot than you can with a single shot. Press the Camera button while you rotate through your desired field of view. The application then digitally stitches the individual photos into a single wide angle shot.

✔ **Sports:** Some digital shots can be blurry if there is fast action. Sports mode compensates for this.

✔ **Night:** This setting lengthens the duration of the shot to help improve the image.

Choose the option that sounds right and snap away.

These modes help when you are taking the shot. You can also edit an image later. You would probably find it easier to do complicated image editing on your desktop computer instead of your phone. However, you can make some edits on your phone and send your photo off right away. Your choice.

Other options

Here are three other ways to enhance your photo options: Flash, Settings, and Effects.

Flash options

Sometimes you need a flash for your photo. Sometimes you need a flash for your photo, but it's not allowed, such as when you're taking images of fish in an aquarium, newborns, or some animals. (Remember what happened to King Kong?) Regardless of the situation, your phone gives you control of the flash. Tap the Settings icon at the top of the viewfinder. This brings up the options seen in Figure 9-6.

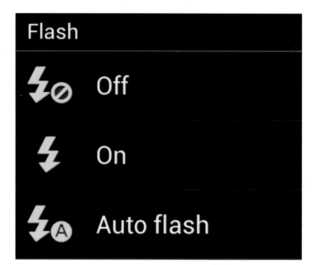

Figure 9-6: Flash options.

You have the options of Off, On, or Auto Flash, which lets the light meter within the camera decide whether a flash is necessary.

Settings options

Tapping the Settings icon on the viewfinder brings up a number of choices:

- ✔ **Photo Size:** You can go up to 13 MP for high image quality, or you can choose a lower resolution to save memory. This option gives you choices.

- ✔ **Burst Shot:** The Samsung Galaxy S 4 offers you the ability to take a fast series of shots instead of just a single shot. If your subject is prone to blinking at just the wrong moment, a series of shots increases the chance of one of the series being good. The phone presents the series right away so you can see if any of them are good.

✔ **Face Detection:** The Samsung Galaxy S 4 can spot a person's face and assumes that you want it to be the place where you focus. Otherwise, if you don't use this mode, the camera may assume that you want whatever is in the center of the viewfinder to be in focus.

✔ **Metering:** If there is no face to detect, you still want the autofocus to work. Using Metering mode lets you tell the camera that you want to focus in on a spot or a zone you select on the viewfinder.

✔ **ISO:** In the olden days of film, the International Standards Organization (ISO) defined a numbering system that would be used for film. Film that was "slow," such as 100 film, was good for bright conditions. The fast film, such as 400 or 800 film, was good for dim conditions. This setting lets classically trained photographers control their settings using old-school terms. The rest of us can just use the Auto setting.

✔ **Anti-Shake:** If too much caffeine is causing your shots to blur, this capability is your answer.

✔ **Auto Night Detection:** This setting automatically takes the steps to make your night images look as good as possible.

Effects options

Back in Figure 9-1, you can see an upwards pointing arrow at the bottom of the screen. That's not just to tell you which way is up. Tapping that arrow brings up a number of effects that you can apply to your image. If you tap the arrow, it brings up a long list of choices. Some examples are shown in Figure 9-7.

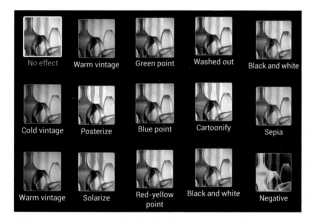

Figure 9-7: Some examples of Effects options.

A personal favorite of mine is the cartoon setting. This takes your image and converts it into a high contrast image that looks like a cartoon, as shown in Figure 9-8.

Figure 9-8: Shooting with the Cartoon option.

Don't use the Cartoon setting for your annual holiday card, or you'll never hear the end of it from your mother-in-law.

Select the option that sounds right and snap away.

If the Galaxy S 4 shooting options listed in the previous section aren't enough, you can find dozens more options. To keep this book from being *Samsung Galaxy S 4 Camera Options For Dummies*, I focus on some highlights and don't try for comprehensive coverage.

Self-Portrait mode

There are estimates (don't ask for citations) that a big chunk of photos taken with cellular phone cameras are self-portraits. I would have a hard time counting all the images friends on Facebook have sent me that involve some-one taking a shot of themselves from their arm's length.

One problem with taking these kinds of pictures is that you cannot be sure that you are centered in the picture. Also, it's hard to be sure that you are pressing the shutter button.

The good news is that your phone has a front-facing camera. All you have to do to take a good self-portrait is tap the self-portrait icon, seen in the following figure. It's in the upper left corner of the viewfinder.

When you tap it, you will suddenly see yourself in the viewfinder! All the settings and options are now at your disposal.

Buddy Share

Your camera has the smarts to recognize your friends from other pictures. Say you tell the camera that a person in one of your images is Fred. Not only will your phone use facial recognition to recognize who is in your picture, but it also makes it easy to share this picture with them by e-mail or SMS text.

You can turn this option on or off from the menu options. When you pull up the menu and tap Buddy Share, a text box appears on the screen next to the faces on the screen. If you tap in one of your contacts, the phone automatically starts looking through your gallery for this individual. It's amazingly good at recognizing your friends!

Digital magnification

If you want to control how much background you see in your shot, Samsung has a slick way to zoom in on a shot. When you're in Camera mode, you can use the phone's Volume buttons to zoom in and out.

✔ **Volume Down:** Press this button to zoom in.

✔ **Volume Up:** Press this button to zoom out.

You might find the digital magnification capability by accident. When you hold the phone horizontally to use as a viewfinder, the Volume Up and Down buttons are on the bottom. This is often where you hold the phone, and you may inadvertently zoom in or out.

The viewfinder tells you how much you have zoomed into the shot, as shown in Figure 9-9.

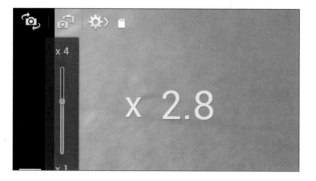

Figure 9-9: The Viewfinder when zooming.

Other cool things

Your phone can do some other cool things, like using the front facing camera to include the image of the photographer into the image from the high resolution camera, build animation into images, and add sound to shots. Explaining all these features goes beyond the scope of this book. I encourage you to play around with some of these features to see which ones you like.

The Digital Camcorder in Your Pocket

Your Samsung Galaxy S 4 Camera application can also function as a digital camcorder.

Starting the camcorder

All you need to do is to put your camera into Camcorder mode. From the camera viewfinder, you tap the icon with the silhouette of a movie camera in the upper right corner and you switch from photographer to videographer.

At this point, recording video automatically starts. You see the notification that says *Rec* in red text and the time code indicating when it started, as shown in Figure 9-10.

It continues recording until you either tap the Stop button, which is the circle with the dark square in the center on the right side of the viewfinder, or the Pause button, which is the button with the parallel slashes in the middle. If you tap the Stop button, the screen reverts back to the still camera.

Stop

Pause

Figure 9-10: Your phone's camcorder viewfinder.

If you press the Pause button while in Camcorder mode, the buttons to the right morph into the options seen in the following figure. Tap the upper button to switch back to the camera. Your other option is to tap the button with the red dot to begin recording again.

Your phone is not only recording the video, but it's also recording the sound. Be careful what you say!

Taking and sharing videos with your camcorder

Just as you share photos you take with the camera, you can immediately share a video, play it, or delete it by tapping the video viewer. Also, the video is immediately saved on your camera. It is stored in the Gallery app (described earlier in this chapter) or is viewable from your Video Player app (covered in Chapter 12).

You can get fancy with some of the settings for your camcorder, but you won't find nearly as many settings as you have for your camera (fortunately!). Two settings, Video Size and Image Stabilization, are available in Settings from the Menu button.

You cannot get to the Settings screen from the Camcorder viewfinder. You must tap the Stop button, which brings you back to Camera mode. From there, tap the Menu button to access Settings.

As with still pictures, you may as well use the highest resolution (or size) unless you're concerned about running out of memory. The highest quality (1920×1080) is the default option, as seen in Figure 9-11.

Use Image Stabilization unless you like the feeling of being seasick.

Figure 9-11: The video options.

 Under most circumstances, you get the best results by leaving the default settings as they are — unless you want to save memory space by reducing your resolution or get really creative by using black-and-white mode effects. However, in this case, I suggest that you change the default settings and select Image Stabilization.

Managing Your Photo Images

After you take some great pictures, you need to figure out what to do with them. Earlier in this chapter, I describe how to send an image immediately to another site or via e-mail. This will likely be the exception, though.

In most cases, it's easier to keep on doing what you were doing and go back to the Gallery application when you have some time to take a look at the images and then decide what to do with them. Your choices include

- ✔ Store them on your phone within the Gallery app.
- ✔ Transfer them to your PC to your photo album application by sending them with e-mail.
- ✔ Store them on an Internet site, like Picasa or Flickr.
- ✔ Print them from your PC.
- ✔ Have them printed and sent to you from a service, such as flicpost (www.flicpost.com).
- ✔ Any combination of the preceding choices.

This section covers how to do each of these options.

Unlike many regular cellphones with a built-in camera, the Galaxy S 4 makes it easy to access these choices. You need to determine the approach or approaches you want to take to keep your images when you want them. The rest of this chapter goes through your options.

Even though the Camera application and the Gallery application are closely related, they are two separate apps. Be sure that you keep straight which application you want to use.

The Gallery Home screen (shown in Figure 9-12) shows how the app first sorts the images on your phone into folders, depending upon when they originated.

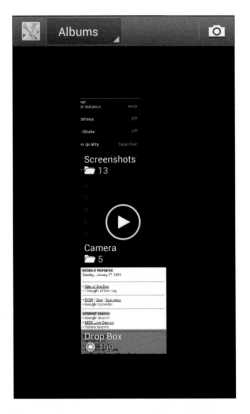

Figure 9-12: The Home screen for the Gallery app.

All your photos from the Camera app are placed in Albums. The application takes a shot at grouping them when a series of pictures or videos are taken about the same time.

To see an image, tap the appropriate folder. If the phones attempt to group them does not work for you, you can tap the Albums setting at the top and choose the Time option. When you do, photos and videos are displayed chronologically. An open folder is shown in Figure 9-13.

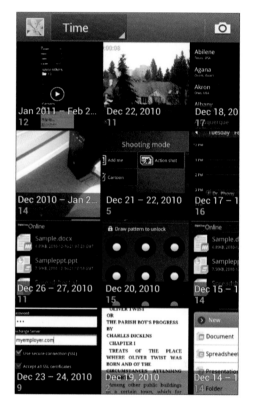

Figure 9-13: The Gallery app in Time mode.

Using Images on Your Phone

In addition to sharing photos from your camera, your Galaxy S 4 phone allows you to use a Gallery photo as wallpaper or as a photo for a contact. And if the fancy shooting settings in the Camera application aren't enough, you can wrangle minor edits — as in cropping or rotating — when you have an image in the Gallery application.

The first step is to find the image that you want in Gallery. If you want to do something to this image other than send it, tap the menu button at the bottom right corner of the screen. This brings up the menu seen in Figure 9-14.

Figure 9-14: Choose from options in Gallery.

- ✔ **Slideshow:** This displays each of the images for a few seconds. You can not only set the speed for transition, but also add music and select among several image transitions.

- ✔ **Copy to Clipboard:** This copies text to an imaginary "clipboard" to be pasted later.

- ✔ **Crop:** Cut away unnecessary or distracting parts of the image. The application creates a virtual box around what it considers to be the main object. You can move the box around the image, but you cannot resize it. You then can either save this cropped image or discard.

- ✔ **Set As:** Make this image your wallpaper or set it as the image for a contact.

- ✔ **Rotate Left/Rotate Right:** These options allow you to rotate the image right or left. This is useful if you turned the camera sideways to get more height in your shot and now want to turn the image to landscape (or vice versa).

- ✔ **Rename:** These options allow you to rotate the image right or left. This is useful if you turned the camera sideways to get more height in your shot and now want to turn the image to landscape (or vice versa).

- ✔ **Details:** See the information on the image: its metadata, which is fixed and cannot change.

Deleting an image

Not all the images on your phone are keepers. This is particularly true if you're using the Continuous option to take a quick series of images. (Read about Burst shot earlier in this chapter.)

When you want to get rid of an image, press and hold the image you want to delete. In a second, an icon appears at the top of the screen in the shape of a trash can.

If you want to delete this image, tap Delete. The camera verifies that this is your intent. After you confirm, the image goes away.

When I say that the photos you delete are gone forever, I do mean *for-ev-er*. Most of us have inadvertently deleted the only copy of an image from a PC or a digital camera. That's not a pleasant feeling, so be careful.

Viewing images on your phone

The Super AMOLED screen on your Galaxy S 4 is a great way to enjoy your photos and share them with family and friends. Depending upon the circumstances, you can view images one at time or as a slideshow.

To see one image at a time, just tap that image. See a series of images by tapping Slideshow, which brings up the next image in chronological order, every four seconds. The Slideshow icon is at the top of the image you're viewing.

Sharing Your Photos

Organizing your photos into albums is important. After you've been taking photos for a while, the job of organizing gets more difficult. You can't remember whether that picture of Johnny was from spring break or Easter. Start putting your pictures in albums sooner rather than later!

You can try to do this in the Gallery, but unfortunately, Gallery isn't really set up to handle your entire photo library.

You have a number of options to get the photos off your phone so you can sort, edit, and organize them. I discuss how to do this with a single image at the beginning of the chapter. It's straightforward to do this with multiple images from within a given folder from the Gallery application.

When you tap Share, the pop-up for the Share options appears (see Figure 9-3). From this pop-up, you select your sharing option. The multiple images are all handled in one group. ***Note:*** This is the same list of sharing options you have for a single photo or video.

As I mention earlier, there is much to be said about storing your digital images on the Internet at an image hosting site like Picasa. If you have a Gmail account, you already have a Picasa account. If not, just register with Picasa at `http://picasa.google.com`.

Picasa isn't the only image-hosting site on the block. Flickr and Windows Live Photo Gallery are also available, to name a few. The advantage of using Picasa is that because the Android operating system and Picasa are both owned by Google, Picasa is already integrated into the system. It's not heroic to use the other sites, but that discussion goes beyond the scope of this book.

The advantages of using Picasa include

- **The storage capacity is huge.** You might have a large memory card in your phone, but the storage available on any image hosting site will dwarf what you have.

    When you upload to Picasa, a copy of the images remains on your phone. You might want to keep it there, or you might want to delete it after you transferred the images successfully to make more room on your phone.

- **It's professionally backed up.** How many of us have lost photos? How many of us have lost phones? 'Nuff said.

- **Picasa is free.** Google offers this service at no charge.

- **Access your images wherever you have Internet access.** Although showing pictures on your phone is great, Gallery isn't set up to host your complete photo library. Picasa can.

- **Others can see your images with links.** Rather than sending the full 8MB image of your kids for each of the 25 images of a birthday party, just send the link. Granny might want all the shots in high resolution. Your college roommate is probably fine with the low resolution images on the Picasa site. No need to clog your old pal's inbox (unless you want to).

- **You control who has access.** Picasa allows you to set up access to selected groups. You can set it so that family has more access than your co-workers, for example.

- **You can order prints of images from your PC.** Picasa allows you to order prints from your PC without the need to transfer the images to another storage medium for you to then trudge down to a store to get prints.

- **There are tools to help you sort your images.** Gallery has limited control over your folders. Picasa, in contrast, can get very granular on how you set up your image folder hierarchy. You can get fancy, or you can keep it very simple. Your choice.

Saving to Picasa is easier than sending an e-mail if you have a Gmail account. Tap the Picasa sharing option, and it will upload that image. I can now create a folder to store the image, edit the image, or share it on other web services. All this is as easy as pie!

Playing Games

In This Chapter

▶ Perusing the games available on the Play Store

▶ Downloading games to your phone

▶ Paying for games

▶ Keeping track of what you've downloaded

Games are the most popular kind of download for smartphones of all kinds. In spite of the focus on business productivity, socializing, and making your life simpler, games outpace all other application downloads. The electronic gaming industry has larger revenues than the movie industry — and has for several years!

The fact of the matter is that your Samsung Galaxy S 4, with its large Super AMOLED screen, makes Android-based games more fun. And because you already have one, maybe you should take a break and concentrate on having fun!

The Play Store Games Category

The Games category of Play Store (shown in Figure 10-1) is huge, and it includes everything from simple puzzles to simulated violence. All games involve various combinations of intellect, skill (either cognitive or motor), and role-playing.

Games

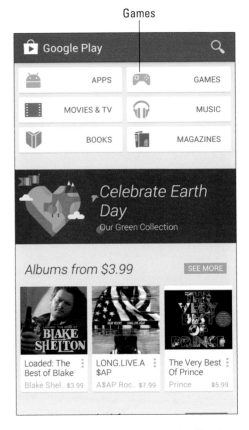

Figure 10-1: The Games button on the Play Store screen.

We could have a lively and intellectually stimulating debate on the merits of games versus applications. For the purposes of this book, the differences between games and apps are as follows:

- Apps and Games are in different sections of the Play Store.
- If a person likes a game, he tends to play it for a while, maybe for a few weeks or even months, and then stop using it. If a person likes an app, they tend to keep on using it.
- People who use their phone for games tend to like to try a wide range of games.

For these reasons, I will pick up where I left off in Chapter 8 and expand on some elements of the Google Play store that are relevant for gamers.

The Games Home tab

When you tap on the Games option in Figure 10-1, you go to the Home screen for Games. If you scroll down, you see many suggested games. This is shown in panorama in Figure 10-2.

Home tab

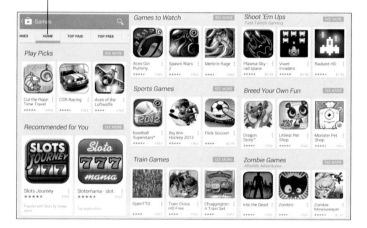

Figure 10-2: The Games Home tab.

If you aren't sure what games you might like to try, don't worry: There are lots of options. The categories shown in Figure 10-2 will probably be different from what you will see. These categories are regularly updated with the latest games.

The Categories tab

If you scroll to the left from the tab that says Home, you see a tab for Categories. These are seen in Figure 10-3.

In the Play Store, Games are divided into the following genres:

✔ **Arcade & Action**

- *Shooting:* Projectiles range from bullets to marshmallows to anti-ballistic missiles.

- *Fighting:* Fighting (combat) games; vary based upon the level of gore.

- *Arcade:* Game room and bar favorites.

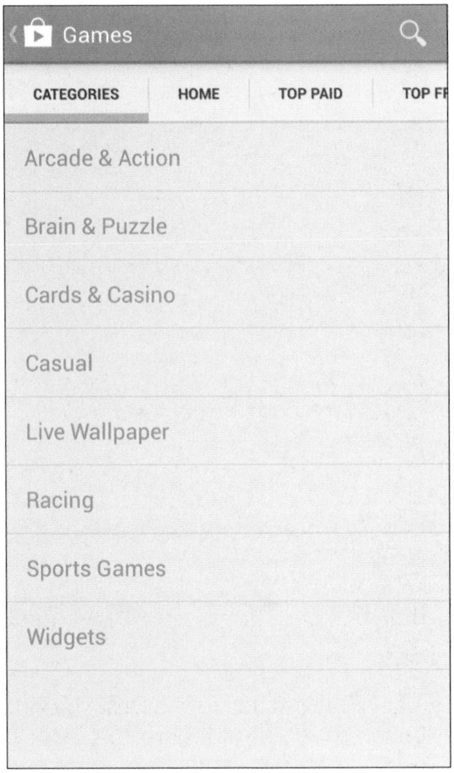

Figure 10-3: The Games Categories tab.

✔ **Brain & Puzzle**

- *Educational:* Enjoyable games that also offer users enhanced skills or information.

- *Puzzles and trivia:* Includes games like Sudoku, word search, and Trivial Pursuit.

- *Strategy and simulation:* Emphasize decision-making skills, like chess; a variety of games with varying levels of complexity and agreement with reality.

✔ **Cards & Casino**

- *Card and board games:* Versions of familiar (and some not-so-familiar) board and card games.

- *Casino games:* Simulations of gambling games; no real money.

✔ **Casual**

Games that you can easily pick up and put aside.

✔ **Live Wallpaper**

These include many games from the other categories, but with the feature that you set them as your wallpaper.

✔ **Racing**

Cars, go-karts, snowboards, jet skis, biplanes, jets, or spacecraft competing with one another.

✔ **Sports Games**

Electronic interpretations of real-world activities that incorporate some of the skill or strategy elements of the original game; vary based upon the level of detail.

✔ **Widgets**

These are the games that automatically appear on your home screen.

Many games appear in more than one category, particularly the ones that are in Live Wallpaper and Widgets.

Each game has a Description page. It is similar to the Description page for apps, but it emphasizes different attributes. Figure 10-4 is an example Description page.

Figure 10-4: A Description page for Flow Free.

When you're in a category that looks promising, look for these roadsigns to help you check out and narrow your choices among similar titles:

- **Ratings/comments:** Gamers love to exalt good games and bash bad ones. The comments here are complimentary, and the overall ranking next to the game name at the top suggests that many others are favorable.

- **Description:** This tells you the basic idea behind the game.

- **What's New:** This section tells what capabilities have been added since the previous release. This is relevant if you have an earlier version of this game.

- **Reviews:** Here is where existing users get to vent their spleen if they do not like the game, or brag about how smart they are for buying it ahead of you. The comments are anonymous, include the date the comment was left, and tell you the kind of device the commenter used. There can be applications that lag on some older devices. However, you have the Galaxy S 4, which has the best of everything (for now).

- **More Games by Developer:** If you have a positive experience with a given game, you may want to check that developer's other games. The More Games by section makes it easier for you to find these other titles.

- **Users Also Viewed/Users Also Installed:** This shows you the other apps that other people who downloaded this app have viewed or downloaded. These are some apps that you may want to check out.

- **Price:** As a tie breaker among similar titles, a slightly higher price is a final indication of a superior game. And because you're only talking a few pennies, price isn't usually a big deal.

Leaving Feedback on Games

The Play Store for applications in general, and games in particular, is a free market. When you come in to the Play Store, your best path to finding a good purchase is to read the reviews of those who have gone before you. Although more than a million users have commented on Angry Birds, most games do not have that kind of following.

One could argue that your opinion would not move the overall rating for a frequently reviewed game like Angry Birds. The same cannot be said for others.

One of the suggestions from Figure 10-2 is the game Zombro in the Zombie genre. The game description for one of the games, Zombro, is seen in Figure 10-5.

Number of times this game has been reviewed.

Figure 10-5: A game description for Zombro.

A Description page before you download it to your phone will have the option to Install, and the feedback areas are grayed out. The Description page after you download it to your phone will offer the options to Open or Uninstall, and the feedback areas are active.

As of this writing, Zombro has been reviewed by 605 gamers. Your opinion matters more for this game than for the heavily reviewed game. After you've downloaded and played a game, you can help make the system work by providing your own review. This section reviews the process, starting at the first screen of the Play Store in Figure 10-1.

1. Tap the Menu icon.

This brings up a pop-up like the image shown in Figure 10-6.

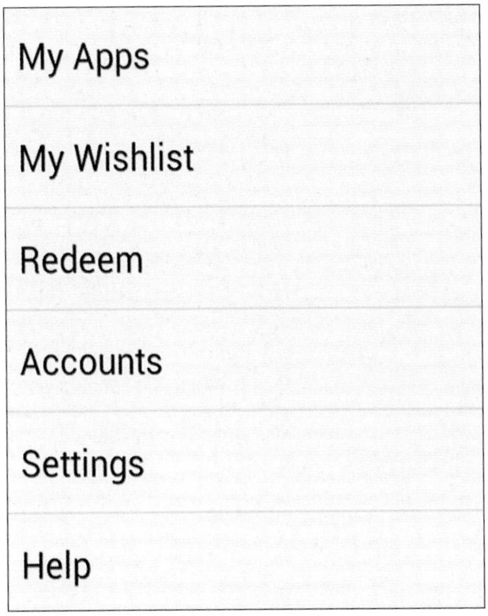

My Apps

My Wishlist

Redeem

Accounts

Settings

Help

Figure 10-6: The Menu pop-up for the
Play Store applications.

2. **Tap My Apps.**

This brings up the applications that you've downloaded, as shown in
Figure 10-7. The Play Store does not distinguish between games and
apps. They're all in the same list.

3. **Tap the game for which you'd like to leave feedback.**

Tapping the title of the game normally brings up the game description
shown in Figure 10-1. After you've downloaded a game, however, a Rate
& Review section appears that lets you leave feedback. See Figure 10-8.

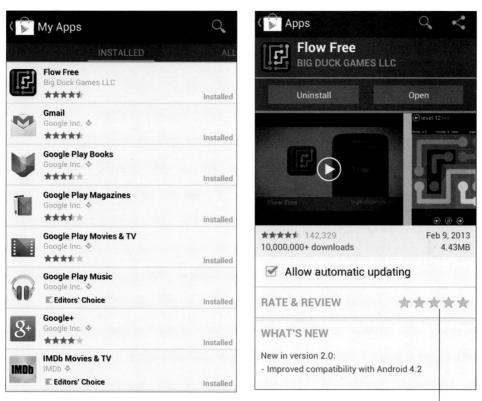

Figure 10-7: Check out your downloads.

Tap to review this app.

Figure 10-8: The Game Description page with space for feedback.

4. **Tap the stars on the screen.**

   This brings up a pop-up screen as shown on the left of Figure 10-9.

5. **Tap the number of stars that you believe this game deserves.**

   The right image of Figure 10-9 shows the result for a five-star review.

   You then make a name for yourself and enter any comments. You cannot enter comments without first choosing the number of stars for this game.

6. When you're done, tap OK.

Your comments are sent to the Play Store for everyone to see. For the sake of the system, make sure that your comments are accurate!

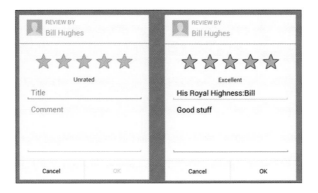

Figure 10-9: The ratings stars pop-up screen before and after entering feedback.

11

Mapping Out Where You Want to Be

· ·

In This Chapter

▶ Deciding what you want to use for navigation

▶ Using what's already on your phone

▶ Using maps safely

· ·

*H*aving a map on your phone is a very handy tool. At the most basic level, you can ask your phone to show you a map for where you plan to go. This is convenient, but only a small part of what you can do.

With the right applications, your Galaxy S 4 phone can do the following:

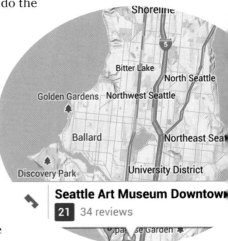

- ✔ Automatically find your location on a map.

- ✔ Give directions to where you want to go:

    - As you drive, using historical driving times

    - As you drive, using real-time road conditions

    - While you walk

    - As you take public transportation

- ✔ Give turn-by-turn directions as you travel:

    - With two-dimensional representations of the road and intersections

    - With three-dimensional representations of the roads, buildings and intersections

- ✔ Tell others where you are.

- ✔ Use the screen on your phone as a viewfinder to identify landmarks as you pan the area (augmented reality).

There are also some mapping applications for the Galaxy S 4 for commercial users, such as CoPilot Mobile Live from ALK Technologies, but I don't cover them in this book.

Figuring Out GPS 101: First Things First

You can't talk smartphone mapping without GPS in the background, which creates a few inherent challenges you need to be aware. First off (and obviously), there is a GPS receiver in your phone. That means the following:

- **Gimme a sec.** Like all GPS receivers, your location-detection system takes a little time to determine your location when you first turn on your phone.

- **Outdoors is better.** Many common places where you use your phone — primarily, within buildings — have poor GPS coverage.

- **Nothing is perfect.** Even with good GPS coverage, location and mapping aren't perfected yet. *Augmented reality,* the option that identifies local landmarks on the screen, is even less perfect.

- **Turn me on.** Your GPS receiver must be turned on for it to work. Sure, turning it off saves battery life but precludes it from working for mapping applications.

- **Keep it on the down-low.** Sharing your location information is of grave concern to privacy advocates. The fear is that a stalker or other villain can access your location information in your phone to track your movements. In practice, there are easier ways to accomplish this goal, but controlling who knows your location is still something you should consider, particularly when you have applications that share your location information. See the section, "Letting Others Know Where You Are," later in this chapter.

Good cellular coverage has nothing to do with GPS coverage. The GPS receiver in your phone is looking for satellites; cellular coverage is based upon antennas mounted on towers or tall buildings.

Mapping apps are useful, but they also use more battery life and data than many other applications. Be aware of the impact on your data usage and battery life. Leaving mapping applications active is convenient, but it can also be a drain on your battery and your wallet if you do not pay attention to your usage and have the wrong service plan.

Practically Speaking: Using Maps

The kind of mapping application that's easiest to understand is one that you open the application, and it presents a local map. Depending upon the model of your phone, you will have a mapping applications preloaded, such as

Google Maps, TeleNav, or VZ Navigator. These are found both on your Home screen and in your Application list.

It's not a large leap for a smartphone to offer directions from your GPS-derived location to somewhere you want to go in the local area. These are standard capabilities found in each of these applications.

This section describes Google Maps and Google Maps Navigation; these are both free and might come preinstalled on your phone. Other mapping applications that might come with your phone, such as Bing Maps or TeleNav, have similar capabilities, but the details will be a bit different. Or, you might wish to use other mapping applications. That's all fine. Take a look at the descriptions and the prices in the Play Store and get the solution that best meets your needs.

As a rule, free navigation applications, like Google Maps Navigation use historical averages for travel times. The applications that charge a modest monthly fee (between $5 and $10 monthly), like VZ Navigator, have real-time updates that avoid taking you on congested routes. So if you depend on your mapping app to get where you're going on a regular basis, you might find it worth your while to spend money for a paid app.

In addition to the general-purpose mapping applications that come on your phone, hundreds of mapping applications are available that can help you find a favorite store, navigate waterways, or find your car in a crowded parking lot. For example, Navigon and TCS offer solutions that base their navigation on real-time traffic conditions and give you-turn-by-turn directions using three-dimensional images of the neighborhoods in which you are driving.

As nice as mapping devices are, they're too slow to tell you to stop looking at them and avoid an oncoming car. If you can't control yourself in the car and need to watch the arrow on the map screen move, do yourself a favor and let someone else drive. If no one else is available to drive, be safe and don't use the navigation service on your phone in the car.

The most basic way to use a map is to bring up the Google Maps application. The icon for launching this app is shown here.

The first screen that you see when you tap the Maps icon is a street map with your location. Figure 11-1 shows an example of a map when the phone user is in the Seattle area.

The Local icon

Figure 11-1: You start where you are.

The location of the user is a blue arrow head at the center of the map. The resolution of the map in the figure starts at about one mile square. You can see other parts of the map by placing a finger on the map and dragging away from the part of the map that you want to see. That brings new sections of the map onto the screen.

Turn the phone to change how the map is displayed. Depending on what you're looking for, a different orientation might be easier.

Changing map scale

A resolution of one square mile will work under some circumstances to help you get oriented in an unfamiliar place. But sometimes it helps to zoom out to get a broader perspective, or zoom in to help you find familiar landmarks, like a body of water or a major highway.

To get more real estate onto the screen, use the pinch motion as discussed in Chapter 2. This shrinks the size of the map and brings in more of the map around where you're pinching. If you need more real estate on the screen, you can keep pinching until you get more and more map. After you have your bearings, you can return to the original resolution by double-tapping the screen.

On the other hand, a scale of one square mile might not be enough. To see more landmarks, use the stretch motion to zoom in. The stretch motion expands the boundaries of the place where you start the screen. Continue stretching and stretching until you get the detail that you want. Figure 11-2 shows a street map both zoomed in and zoomed out. The map on the left is zoomed in in Satellite view. The map on the right is zoomed out in Terrain view.

Zoomed-in image   Panned-out image

Figure 11-2: A street image zoomed in and zoomed out.

The app gives you the choice of satellite view or terrain view by tapping the Layers button on the bottom-right-hand corner of the map. This brings up a pop-up similar to what is seen in Figure 11-3.

Bring up the Satellite view by tapping Satellite. You get the Terrain view by tapping Terrain. You can also bring up other views that are useful to you, including transit routes and bicycling paths. I show you some of the other options later in this chapter.

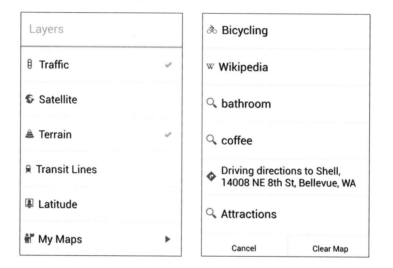

Figure 11-3: The Layers pop-up.

If you're zooming in and can't find where you are on the map, tap the dot-surrounded-by-a-circle icon (refer to Figure 11-1 for the centering icon). It moves the map so that you're in the center.

Finding nearby services

Most searches for services fall into a relatively few categories. Your Maps application is set up to find what you're most likely to seek. By tapping the Local icon (refer to Figure 11-1), you're offered a quick way to find the services near you, such as restaurants, coffee shops, bars, hotels, attractions, ATMs, and gas stations, as shown in Figure 11-4.

Just tap one of the topical icons, and your phone performs a search of businesses in your immediate area. The results come back as a regular Google search with names, addresses, and distances from your location. An example is shown in Figure 11-5.

Then tap one of the options to see more details on that business; see the result in Figure 11-6.

In addition to the location and reviews are three icons and other relevant information:

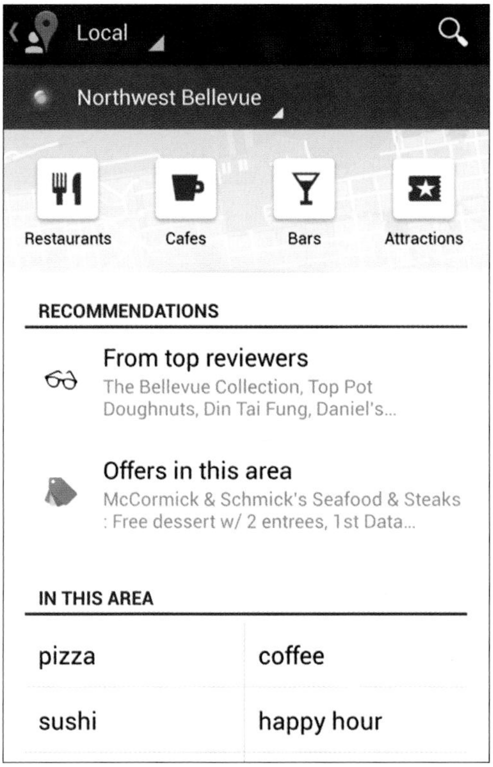

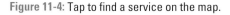

Figure 11-4: Tap to find a service on the map. 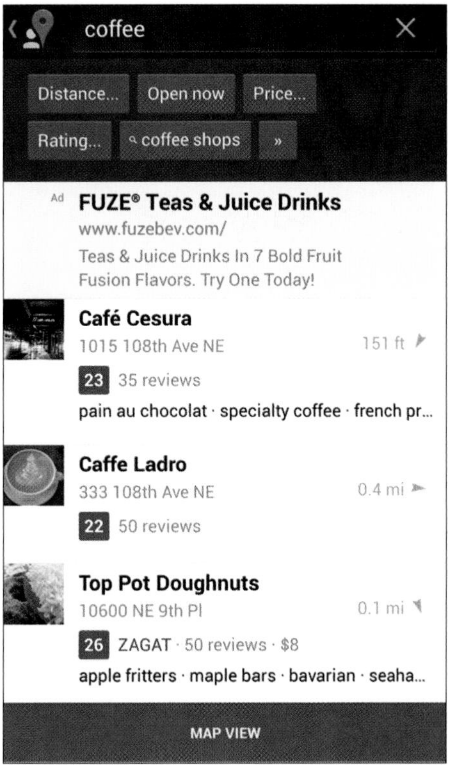   Figure 11-5: The results of a service selection.

⤔ **Map:** Tap to see a map of where you are in relation to this business

⤔ **Directions:** Tap to get turn-by-turn directions from your location to this business

You might need to download Google Maps Navigation to your phone to get the turn-by-turn directions. This is a free app from the Play Store. For more on how to download applications, read Chapter 8.

⤔ **Call:** Tap this to call the business.

⤔ More options, which include

* *Street View:* See the location in Google Street View. As shown at the bottom of Figure 11-6, Street View shows a photo of the street address for the location you entered.

* *Reviews:* This includes all kinds of information about how people have experienced this location.

* *More:* Run another Google search on this business to get additional information, such as reviews from other parts of the web.

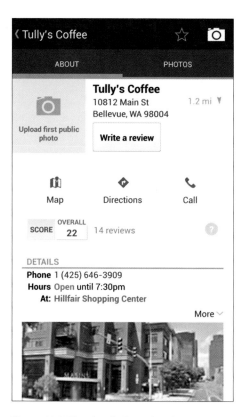

Figure 11-6: The detailed results of a service selection.

Just how deeply you dive into using this information is up to you. In any case, having this kind of information when you're visiting an unfamiliar location is handy.

Getting and Using Directions

You probably want to get directions from your map application. I know I do. You can get directions in a number of ways, including

- ✔ Tap the Search text box and enter the name or address of your location: for example, **Seattle Space Needle** or **742 Evergreen Terrace, Springfield, IL**

- ✔ Tap the Search icon of the Device Function keys and enter a location.

- ✔ Tap the Services icons (refer to Figure 11-2), tap the Attractions icon (refer to Figure 11-4), and select your location.

Any of these methods lead you to the map showing your location, as shown in Figure 11-7.

Figure 11-7: A street map search result.

It might seem intuitive that when you search for a specific attraction (such as the Seattle Space Needle), you get only the Seattle Space Needle. However, that's too simple. Google Map gives you several choices. Tap the "B" to get more detailed results (refer to Figure 11-7).

To get directions, tap the Directions icon. This brings up the pop-up screen shown in Figure 11-8.

Figure 11-8: Your direction options, from original location to the target.

This gives you the options of

✓ **Driving:** Turn-by-turn directions as you drive from where you are to the destination

✓ **Public Transportation:** This option tells you how to get to your destination by taking public transportation using published schedules.

✓ **Cycling:** This option is for the cyclists among us and includes bike trails in addition to city streets.

✓ **Walking Navigation:** Turn-by-turn directions as you walk to your destination

For each of these options, you can either use the options at the bottom of the screen to

✓ **Navigation:** Rather than show you a map, this puts you in a navigation app that monitors where you are as you travel and tells you what to do next.

✔ **Get Directions:** Sequential directions, as shown in Figure 11-9, but Get Directions doesn't tell you when to turn.

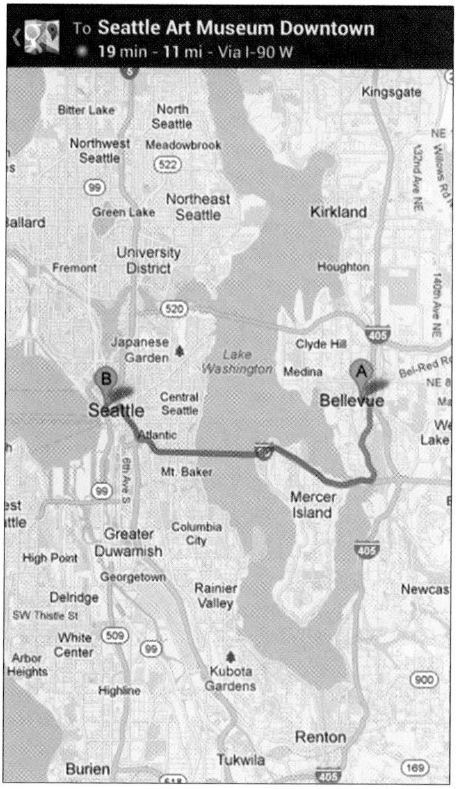

Figure 11-9: Step-by-step directions to the target.

Some Navigation apps are premium and have a monthly charge. If you do not mind and this is what you want, no problem. If you are in a hurry, it is easy to miss that a fee is involved and be surprised later.

Letting Others Know Where You Are

The Maps application can let you know where you are, but there are also situations where either you want your location to be shared with others or others insist on knowing where you are. For example, you might want to let friends know your location when you're planning to meet at an amusement park. Likewise, parents might insist on knowing the location of their children as a condition for having a cellular phone.

Your Samsung Galaxy S 4 supports these capabilities with the Google Latitude application. This app might or might not be on your phone. It is readily available from the Play Store for free, though; see Chapter 8.

Before you can see the location of anyone besides yourself, you have to invite that person. The process is as follows:

1. **Open the Google Maps app.**

    This brings up a map (refer to Figure 11-1).

2. **Tap the Layers icon to launch the Latitude service.**

    The Layer pop-up opens as shown in Figure 11-10.

3. **Tap Latitude.**

    Before Latitude lets you get too far, it brings up the screen shown in Figure 11-11 to request your permission to share your location.

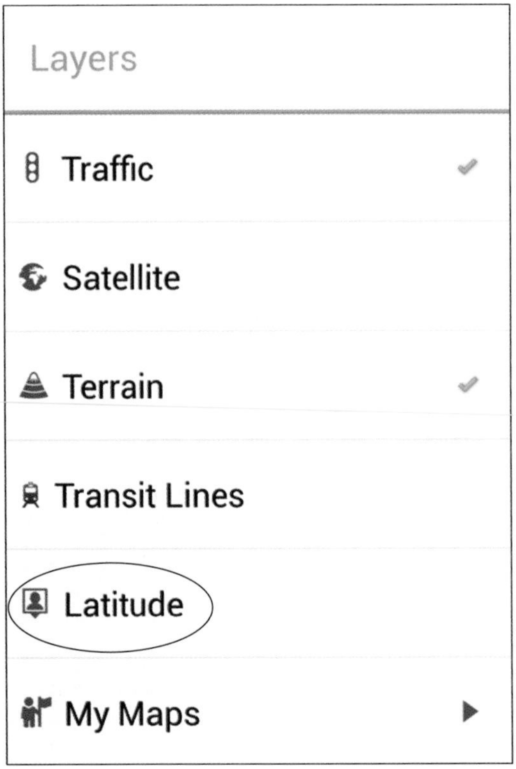

Layers
⛽ **Traffic** ✓
🌐 **Satellite**
⛰ **Terrain** ✓
🚆 **Transit Lines**
(📍 **Latitude**)
🚶 **My Maps** ▶

Figure 11-10: The Layers pop-up with Latitude highlighted.

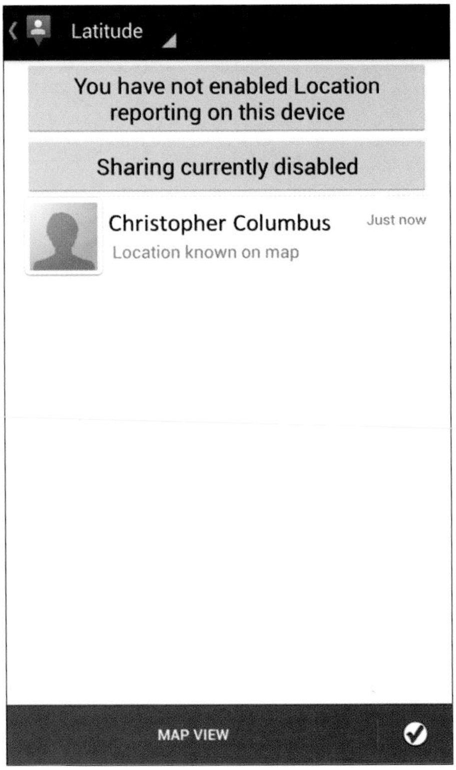

〈 📍 Latitude ◢

You have not enabled Location reporting on this device

Sharing currently disabled

Christopher Columbus   Just now
Location known on map

MAP VIEW ✓

Figure 11-11: The Latitude Home screen with a permissions reminder.

This app makes sure that you know what you are getting yourself into. If you're worried about a stalker, think twice about enabling this feature. Of all the applications I know, this is one that hands over your information (and your current location) on a silver platter. As a result, the app goes out of its way to make sure that you know what you are doing and only share your location information the way you intend.

4. Tap You Have Not Enabled Location Reporting on this device.

Tapping this button brings up the screen shown in Figure 11-12. Tap all the boxes if you want to enable this app.

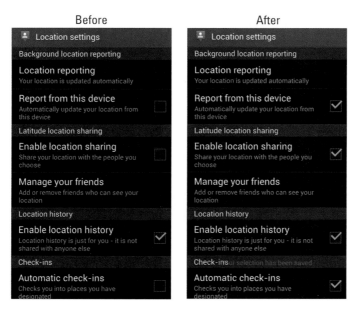

Figure 11-12: The Background Location Reporting Permissions page.

After you have changed your permissions, return to the map. You should see the Latitude Home screen with your name. The reminders are gone. At the bottom, you'll see the icons shown in Figure 11-13.

5. Tap the Add Friends icon shown in Figure 11-13.

Tapping this icon brings up all your contacts.

6. Tap the Select from Contacts hyperlink to invite friends or family from your Contacts list.

At this point, you have the ability to know the location of all your friends (or at least the location of their phones) in addition to having the ability to have turn-by-turn direction on how to meet up with them.

Figure 11-13: The Latitude Home screen.

Playing Music and Video

Most smartphones have built-in digital music players. Having a single device that you can use as a phone and as a source of music is quite convenient because then you need only one device rather than two, and you eliminate cords for charging and separate headphones for listening. Your Samsung Galaxy S 4 is no exception. You can play digital music files and podcasts all day and all night on your phone.

In addition, by virtue of the Super AMOLED screen on your Galaxy S 4 smartphone, your phone makes for an excellent handheld video player. Just listen on the headset and watch on the screen, whether you have a short music video or a full-length movie.

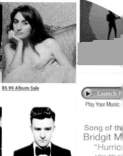

To boot, your Galaxy S 4 phone comes with applications for downloading and listening to music as well as downloading and watching videos. These apps are very straightforward, especially if you've ever used a CD or a DVD player. In a sense, they're even easier than using a VCR — no need to set the clock!

Being Mindful of Carrier Quirks

The only possible pitfall for you playing music and videos is that each carrier has its own spin: Some cellular carriers want you to use their music store, and some give you the freedom to enjoy the flexibility that comes with owning an Android-based phone. You can use the basic multimedia tools that come with the phone, or download the myriad of options that you have via the Play Store. (Read all about the Play Store in Chapter 8.)

However, other cellular carriers, and Samsung, offer you the Samsung Hub, an all-in-one tool for managing your multimedia options, which I discuss in this chapter.

To keep things straight, read on to see your options regardless of what cellular carrier you use, including the use of the basic multimedia applications that came with your phone. Lots and lots of options for entertainment exist out there. The truth is that there isn't that much difference among them when it comes to playing. The differences lie in price and selection.

Therefore, I cover the basic functions, but I encourage you to find the entertainment that you prefer. Trust me. It's out there somewhere. A good mainstream option is the Samsung Hub, which I introduce you to in this chapter. However, do not worry about loyalty to this service. Find the music you like and subscribe to as many services as it takes to bring you joy.

Remember, the whole point is about enjoyment. Enjoy yourself!

Getting Ready to be Entertained

Regardless of the model phone that you have, for the app you use for entertainment — and whether you're listing to audio or video — here are some common considerations I need to cover up front.

The first is the use of headsets. Yeah, you use *headphones* with your MP3 player, but your phone uses a *headset*. The vocabulary is more than just semantics, too, because a headset has headphones plus a microphone so you can make and take phone calls.

Secondly, you need to know about connecting your Galaxy S 4 phone to a television and/or stereo. After I talk about that, I cover the issue of licensing multimedia material.

Choosing your headset options

You can use wired or wireless (Bluetooth) headsets with your Samsung Galaxy S 4 phone. Wired headsets are less expensive than Bluetooth headsets, and of course, wired headsets don't need charging, as do the Bluetooth headsets.

On the other hand, you lose freedom of mobility if you're tangled up in wires. And, the battery within Bluetooth headsets last much longer than the battery of your phone.

Wired headsets

At the top of your Galaxy S 4 phone is a headset jack. If you try to use your regular headphone jack in this jack, you'll hear the audio, but the person on the other end of the call may not hear you too because the headphone doesn't come with a microphone. In this case, your phone tries to use the built-in mic as a speakerphone. Depending upon the ambient noise conditions, it may work fine or sound awful. Of course, you can always ask the person you are talking to if they can hear you.

Your phone might come with a wired headset to address that problem. In that case, just plug it in to use the device. The Galaxy S 4 uses ear buds, like the image shown in Figure 12-1.

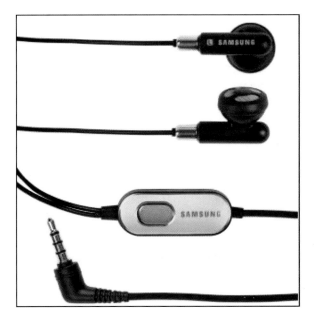

Figure 12-1: A typical wired headset with ear buds and a 3.5mm plug.

Some people dislike ear buds. You can obtain other styles at a number of retail franchises that offer the following options, including

- Around-the-ear headphones that place the speakers on the ear and are held in place with a clip
- A behind-the-neck band that holds around-the-ear headphones in place
- An over-the-head band that places the headphones on the ear

The laws in some regions prohibit the use of headphones while driving. Correcting the officer and explaining that these are really "headsets," and not "headphones" won't help your case if you're pulled over. Even if not explicitly illegal in an area, it's still a bad idea to play music in both ears at a volume that inhibits your ability to hear warnings while driving.

In any case, give yourself some time to get used to any new headset. There is often an adjustment period while you get used to having a foreign object in or around your ear.

Stereo Bluetooth headsets

The other option is to use a stereo Bluetooth headset. Figure 12-2 shows a typical model.

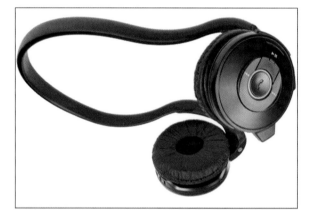

Figure 12-2: A behind-the-neck Bluetooth stereo headset.

A stereo Bluetooth headset is paired the same way as any other Bluetooth headset. (Read how to do this in Chapter 3.) When your Galaxy S 4 phone and the headset connect, the phone recognizes that it operates in stereo when listening to music or videos.

There are also several variations on how to place the headphone part of the headset near your ear with a Bluetooth headset. Be aware that some products on the market are strictly Bluetooth headphones, and not headsets. This means that they don't have a microphone. In this case, you might want to remove your headphones when a call comes in or move the phone near your mouth. Of course, this effort defeats some of the convenience of having a Bluetooth connection.

Connecting to your stereo or TV

You can connect your Galaxy S 4 phone to your stereo. You can also connect your phone to your TV. There are distinct approaches to connection if you are connecting just audio to your stereo or audio and video to your TV.

Connecting to your stereo

Although being able to listen to your music on the move is convenient, it's also nice to be able to listen to your music collection on your home stereo. Your Galaxy S 4 phone presents your stereo with a nearly perfect version of what went in. The sound quality that comes out is limited only by the quality of your stereo.

In addition, you can play the music files and playlists stored on your phone, which can be more convenient than playing CDs. Setting this up involves plugging the 3.5mm jack from the cable in Figure 12-3 into the 3.5mm jack available on newer stereos.

Figure 12-3: The patch cable with 3.5mm plugs.

When you play the music as you do through a headset, it will play through your stereo. Although each stereo system is unique, the correct setting for the selector knob is AUX. You will be entertained. Enjoy yourself.

Connecting to your TV

You can also play videos from your phone on your TV — but you need a few things. First, you need to get a Samsung HDTV Smart Adapter, shown in Figure 12-4.

Figure 12-4: The Samsung HDTV Smart Adapter.

The list price is about $25, but you can find this on sale on the Internet for a few dollars less. After you have one of these, you need to get a few more things together.

For starters, you need a standard HDMI cable. If you have an HDTV, this is a standard cable. If you do not have one handy, you can borrow one from your game console. I'm sure your kids won't mind as long as you put things back the way you found them when you are done.

Finally, you need to have on hand your USB cable/charger. This is the one that you use to charge your phone. This set-up draws more power than your battery can safely deliver, so you need to connect the charging cable. However, instead of plugging into the bottom of your phone as if you are recharging it, follow these steps:

1. **Get together your phone, charger/cable, HDTV Smart Adapter, and HDMI cable near your TV.**

   I'll show you how to connect the components working from the TV to the phone. This is an arbitrary choice. You could work the other way or start in the middle.

2. **Connect the HDMI cable to an open HDMI port on your TV.**

   If you are not disconnecting an existing HDMI cable, connect one end of the HDMI cable to an open port on your HDTV. Remember the name or number of that port.

3. **Plug the other end of the HDMI cable into the HDMI port on the HDTV Smart Adapter.**

4. **Plug the micro USB from the charger into the HDTV Smart Adapter.**

   This is the only place where things could go wrong. You are used to plugging the micro USB into the bottom of your phone. In this case, you plug it into the HDTV Smart Adapter.

5. **Plug the Micro USB from the HDTV Smart Adapter into the bottom of your phone.**

6. **Turn on your TV and direct it to this port.**

   I suggested that you remember the name or number of the HDMI port you connected on your TV. If you forgot, find it now.

   You should now see and hear everything that takes place on your phone on your TV. Start the video application and enjoy! I show you how to use the Video Player application later in this chapter.

Your phone can't switch mid-video from playing on your phone to playing on your TV. If you happen to be in the middle of your movie, you need to shut down the Video Player application and restart the app and the movie.

Licensing your multimedia files

It's really quite simple: You need to pay the artist to listen to music or watch video with integrity. Many low-cost options are suitable for any budget. Depending upon how much you plan to listen to music, podcasts, or watch videos, you can figure out what's the best deal.

Stealing music or videos is uncool. Although it might be technically possible to play pirated music and videos on your phone, it's stealing. Don't do it.

You can buy or lease music, podcasts, or videos. In most cases, you pay for them with a credit card. And depending upon your cellular carrier, you might be allowed to pay for them on your monthly cellular bill.

Listening up on licensing

Here are the three primary licensing options available for music files and podcasts:

- **By the track:** Pay for each song individually. Buying a typical song costs about 79 to 99 cents. Podcasts, which are frequently used for speeches or lectures, can vary dramatically in price.

- **By the album:** Buying an album isn't a hold-over from the days before digital music. Music artists and producers create albums with an organization of songs that offer a consistent feeling or mood. Although many music-playing applications allow you to assemble your own playlist, an album is created by professionals. In addition, buying a full album is often less expensive than on a per-song basis. You can get multiple songs for $8 to $12.

✔ **With a monthly pass:** The last option for buying audio files is the monthly pass. For about $15 per month, you can download as much music as you want from the library of the service provider.

If you let your subscription with a monthly pass provider lapse, you won't be able to listen to the music from this library.

In addition to full access to the music library, some music library providers offer special services to introduce you to music that's similar to what you've been playing. These services are a very convenient way to learn about new music. If you have even a small interest in expanding your music repertoire, these services are an easy way to do it.

Whether buying or renting is most economical depends on your listening/ viewing habits. If you don't plan to buy much, or you know specifically what you want, you might save some money by paying for all your files individually. If you're not really sure what you want, or you like a huge variety of things, paying for monthly access might make better sense for you.

Licensing for videos

The two primary licensing options available for videos are

✔ **Rental:** This option is similar to renting a video from a store. You can view the video as many times as you like within 24 hours from the start of the first play. In addition, the first play must begin within a defined period, such as a week, of your downloading it. Most movies are in the $3 to $5 range.

✔ **Purchase:** You have a license to view the file as frequently as you want, for as long as you want. The purchase cost can be as low as $12, but is more typically in the $15 range.

At the moment, there are no sources for mainstream Hollywood films that allow you to buy a monthly subscription and give you unlimited access to their film library. This can change at any time, so watch for announcements.

Enjoying Basic Multimedia Capabilities

Regardless of the version of your Galaxy S 4, some basic multimedia capabilities are common across the different phones. Figure 12-5 shows a typical Application list with multimedia options.

Your phone comes with the Music Player and Video Player applications preloaded, and you might have other multimedia applications as well, depending upon your carrier.

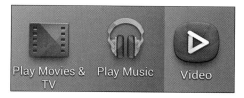

Figure 12-5: The Application list, showing multimedia apps.

Don't worry about storage capacity for your music. A very rough estimate is that a gigabyte (GB) of storage will store 120 hours of music. The memory cards that come with your phone can store 16 or more gigabytes. You can also buy memory cards these days that can store 64GB and cost about $90 (retail $150). There are limits on storing videos, however. Roughly, one full-length movie takes up 1GB. Don't bother trying to put your entire video collection on your phone unless you have a very small collection.

Grooving with the Music Player app

The Music Player app allows you to play music and audio files. The first step is to obtain music and audio files for your phone.

Some ways to acquire music and/or recordings for your phone are

- Buy and download tracks from an online music store.
- Load them on your MicroSD memory card from the digital music collection on your PC.
- Receive them as an attachment via e-mail or text message.
- Receive them from another device connected with a Bluetooth link.
- Record them on your phone.

Buying from an online music store

The most straightforward method of getting music on your phone is from an online music store. You can download a wide variety of music from dozens of mainstream online music stores. The Play Store is an option. In addition to apps, it has music and video.

Also pre-installed on your phone is the Samsung Hub. This app is a music and video store that comes with a mainstream collection. Other well-known sites include Rhapsody, Amazon MP3, VEVO, and last.fm.

In addition, many more specialty or "boutique" stores provide more differentiated offerings than you can get from the mass-market stores. For example, MAQAM offers Middle Eastern music (www.maqammp3.com).

The details for acquiring music among the online stores vary from store to store. Ultimately, there are more similarities than differences. As an example of when you know what you want, what you really, really want, here's how to find and download the song "Wannabe" by the Spice Girls. I'm using Amazon MP3. If you don't have Amazon MP3 in your Application list, you would start by loading that app on your phone, as I describe in Chapter 8. When you open it, you see the screen shown in Figure 12-6.

Figure 12-6: The Amazon MP3 home screen.

From here, you can search for music by album, song, or music genre. Amazon MP3 offers a different free music track and an album at a deep discount every day.

Now to search for the song you want:

1. **Enter the relevant search information in the Amazon MP3 Search field.**

   In this case, I'm searching for "Wannabe" by the Spice Girls. The result of the search for songs looks like Figure 12-7.

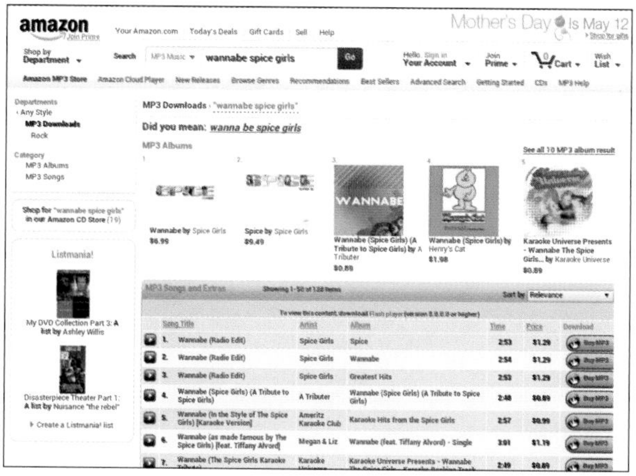

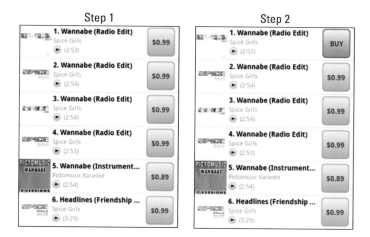

Figure 12-7: Search results for a song at the Amazon MP3 store.

The search results come up with all kinds of options, including albums, individual tracks, similar songs, other songs from the same artist. Be ready for these options.

2. **To purchase the track, tap twice on the price.**

The left screen in Figure 12-8 shows the price. When you tap once on the price, you get a confirmation message to be sure that you want to buy the download; the price is replaced with a Buy icon, as shown on the right in Figure 12-8. To buy, tap Buy.

Figure 12-8: Tap twice to buy.

3. **Sign in with your account information, as shown in Figure 12-9.**

Unless you're going to subsist on the free MP3 files you can get from this site, you need to pay. To pay for files at an online music store, you need an account and a credit card. This process is similar, if not identical, to signing up for Play Store (see Chapter 8). You need your e-mail account, a password, and in some cases, an account name. In the case of Amazon MP3, you already have an account if you have an account with Amazon. If not, you'll be asked to create an account.

After you enter this information, the file will automatically begin downloading to your phone, and a progress screen (as shown in Figure 12-10) lets you know when you're finished.

The song is now loaded on your phone. When you open the music player, it is ready for you to play.

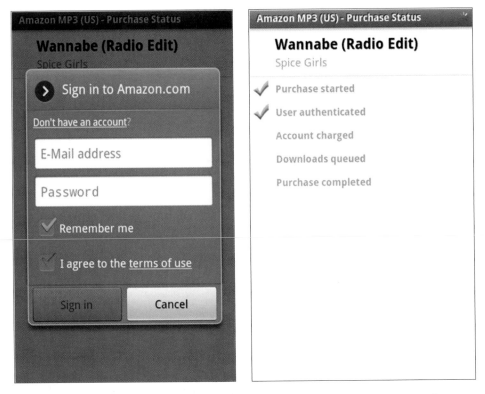

Figure 12-9: The account sign-in screen for the Amazon MP3 store.

Figure 12-10: The screen for downloading tracks from the Amazon MP3 store.

Loading digital music from your PC

In addition to acquiring music files from an online music store, you can also transfer digital music tracks stored on your PC.

The challenge is choosing the method to transfer files from your PC to your phone. If you plan to download one or a few files, using e-mail is most convenient. (The next section covers the receiving music files via e-mail as an attachment.) If you plan to move a large music library from your PC to your phone, however, the e-mail approach is too cumbersome. Instead, load the memory card that resides within your phone by connecting it to your PC.

You'll need to use an adapter — a card reader — that allows you to insert your MicroSD memory in a holder with a standard USB connection. An image of one such adapter with the memory card is in Figure 12-11. The actual size of the card is about as big as the fingernail on your pinky.

Figure 12-11: A Micro SD card and a USB adapter.

Each model of phone has an SD card that comes with it. You can buy cards with larger capacity if you wish. Prices for these memory cards have been dropping, but as a ballpark, a 4GB card will run you $5, $8 for 8GB, $15 for 16GB, and $25 for 32GB. Expect to pay more at a cellular carrier's retail store, however.

If you've ever used a thumb drive to transfer a file from one PC to another, you'll find the process similar when you're copying music files to your phone via the MicroSD card. These steps are as follows:

1. **Turn off your phone.**

2. **Remove the back of your phone, as described in Chapter 2.**

3. **Remove the MicroSD card from your phone.**

   The memory card lies flat in its slot. To remove it, use a fingernail to push it further into its slot. The spring ejects it slightly from the slot.

4. **Insert your memory card into your adapter.**

5. **Plug your adapter into your PC.**

   When you plug in the USB MicroSD Adapter into a USB port, your PC recognizes it as just another thumb drive (a removable disk) and asks you what you want to do. A typical choice pop-up menu for a PC is shown in Figure 12-12. The actual screen you see depends upon how your PC is set up, of course.

Figure 12-12: A typical AutoPlay pop-up screen on a PC.

6. **Click Open Folder to View Files.**

   This opens a window with the files on your MicroSD card.

7. **On your PC, open the folder with your digital music and copy the files you want to your MicroSD card.**

   Don't worry about which folder to place the files. Your phone is happy to do that for you.

8. **After all the files are copied, eject the adapter MicroSD card from your PC.**

9. **Remove the MicroSD card from your adapter and put it back in your phone.**

10. **Turn on your phone.**

   Your phone sees these new files, knows that they are audio files, and organizes them for you when you open up the Music Player app. Done.

Receiving music as an attachment

As long as you comply with your license agreement, you can e-mail or text a music file as an attachment to anyone, including yourself. Simply send yourself an e-mail from your PC with the desired music file. You then open the e-mail and text on your phone, as shown in Figure 12-13.

Your phone can play music files that come in any of the following formats: FLAC, WAV, Vorbis, MP3, AAC, AAC+, eAAC+, WMA, AMR-NB, AMR-WB, MID, AC3, and XMF.

Figure 12-13: A text with an attached music file.

All you need to do is tap Save, and the file is saved on your phone and accessible from the Music Player app. Done.

Recording sounds on your phone

No one else might think your kids' rendition of "Happy Birthday" is anything special, but you probably treasure it. In fact, there is a recording app that comes with your phone. The icon for the Voice Recorder is shown here.

In general, there is a simple record button that creates a sound file when you stop recording. The sound quality might not be the best, but what you record can be just as important or entertaining as what you buy commercially. Your phone treats all audio files the same and is playable on your Music Player.

Playing downloaded music

To play your music, open the Music Player application; see the following figure.

Just tap that icon. The first screen that you see sorts your music files into a number of categories, as shown in Figure 12-14.

Figure 12-14: Music categories for the Music Player app.

The categories include

 **Playlists:** Some digital music stores bundle songs into playlists, such as Top Hits from the 50s. You can also create your own playlists for groups of songs that are meaningful to you.

 **Recent:** This list is for the songs you most recently added to your collection.

 **Artists:** This category lists all songs from all the albums from a given artist.

- ✓ **Albums:** Tapping this category places all your songs into an album with which the song is associated. When you tap the album, you see all the songs you've purchased, whether one song or all the songs from that album, as shown in Figure 12-15.

- ✓ **Songs:** This lists all your song files in alphabetical order.

- ✓ **Genres:** This category separates music into music genres, such as country and western, or heavy metal.

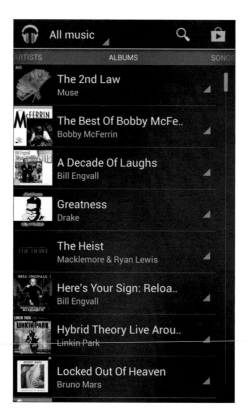

Figure 12-15: Album sort for the Music Player app.

These categories are useful when you have a large number of files. To play a song, an album, or a genre, open that category and tap the song, playlist, album, artist, or genre, and the song will start playing.

Adding songs as ringtones and alarms

Here's how to add a song as a ringtone or alarm. The first step is to open a contact. A generic contact is seen in Figure 12-16. Refer to Chapter 6 if you have any questions about contacts.

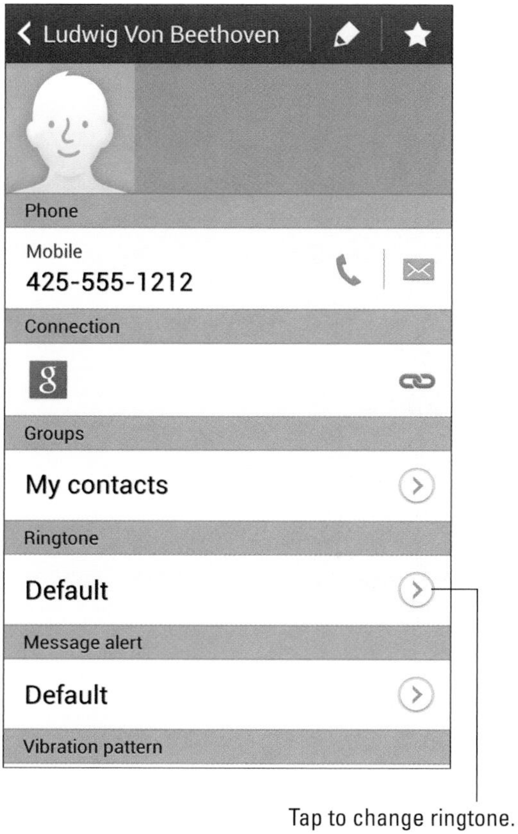

Tap to change ringtone.

Figure 12-16: A typical contact for a Baroque composer.

Follow these steps:

1. Tap the arrow key across from the Default Ringtone.

This will bring up a list of ringtones shown in Figure 12-17.

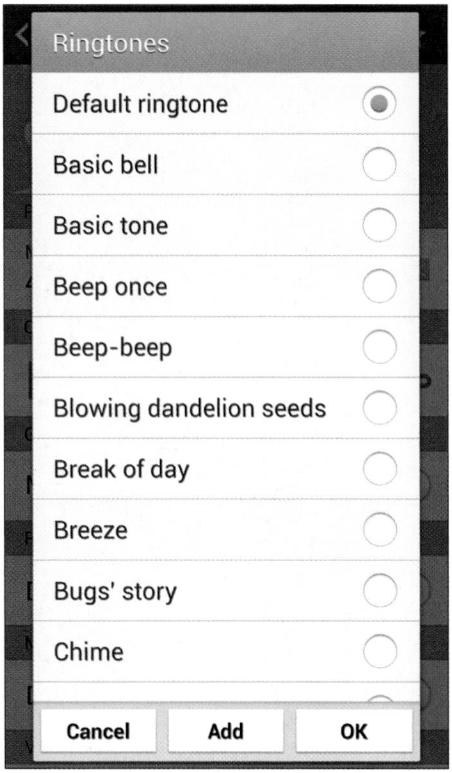

Ringtones	
Default ringtone	●
Basic bell	○
Basic tone	○
Beep once	○
Beep-beep	○
Blowing dandelion seeds	○
Break of day	○
Breeze	○
Bugs' story	○
Chime	○

| Cancel | Add | OK |

Figure 12-17: Basic ringtones.

A quick scan finds that *Ode to Joy* is not among the options that come with your phone. To use a music file as a ringtone, find the Add button on the bottom of the pop-up.

2. Tap Add.

This brings up a pop-up listing places where you can find music files, as seen in Figure 12-18.

3. Tap Choose Music Track and then tap Always.

This brings up your list of songs as shown in Figure 12-19.

4. Highlight the song you want and tap OK.

From now on, when you hear this song, you know it will be your friend Ludwig.

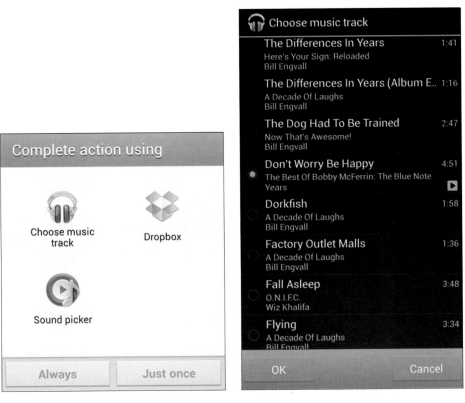

Figure 12-18: The Complete Action Using pop-up.

Figure 12-19: The Music Player app's Choose Music Track options.

Creating playlists

Next to each song or album is a gray arrowhead pointing down and to the right, as seen in Figure 12-15. If you tap on this, you get a pop-up that offers you several options. One is to create a playlist or add to a playlist. Tap the playlist option. You will be asked to name a new playlist or open an existing one.

Figure 12-20 shows a list of playlists. If you want to add that song to an existing playlist, tap the name of that playlist, and it's added. The next time you select that playlist, it's there.

Jamming to Internet radio

If you have not tried Internet radio, you should definitely consider it. The basic idea is that you enter information on your current music favorites, and these services play music that is similar. Pandora and Slacker Radio are two of the best known services of this type and one or the other may have been pre-installed on your phone. If not, they are available for download from the Play Store. Figure 12-21 shows some of the 9,000 Internet radio apps in the Play Store.

These are a great way to learn about new songs and groups that may appeal to you. The service streams music to your phone for you to enjoy. You can buy the track if you choose.

Streaming audio files uses a large amount of data over time. This may be no problem if you have an unlimited or even large data service plan. Otherwise, your "free" Internet radio service can wind up costing you a lot. You are best off using Wi-Fi.

Figure 12-20: Playlists on my phone.

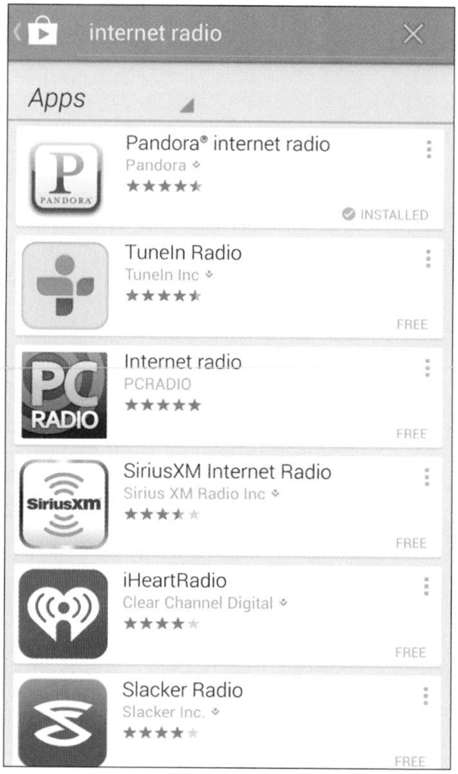

Figure 12-21: Some Internet radio options in the Play Store.

Looking at your video options

The Music Player app allows you to play music files. Similarly, you use the Video Player to play video options. The Video Player is in your Application list and might even be on your Home page. In most ways, playing videos is the same as playing audio with a few exceptions:

✔ Many people prefer to buy music, but renting is more typical for videos.

✔ Video files are usually, but not always, larger.

Otherwise, similar to music files, you can acquire videos for your phone from an online video store, and you need to have an account and pay for the use. In addition, you can download video files to your phone, and the Video Player will play them like a VCR or DVD player.

There are three categories for your videos. These are seen in panorama in Figure 12-22.

✔ Movies

✔ TV Shows

✔ Personal Videos

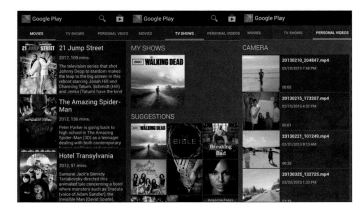

Figure 12-22: Google Play video categories.

In Chapter 9, I covered how to use the digital camcorder on your phone. You can watch any video you've shot on your phone from the Google Play application and scrolling over to the Personal Video section.

Your phone can show the following video formats: MPEG-4, WMV, AVI/DivX, MKV, and FLV.

To play your video, simply tap the name of the file, as shown in Figure 12-22. The app begins showing the video in landscape orientation. The controls that pop up when you tap the screen are similar to a VCR or DVD player.

Skyping with Your Galaxy S 4

On the topic of multimedia, this is a good time to bring up a very popular capability: video chat. Video chatting, long predicted as the next great thing by Ma Bell since the 1960s, is finally coming on strong. The good news is that the multimedia capabilities built into your phone make your Galaxy S 4 the ideal platform for video chats.

This section within the chapter explores how to use Skype for Android. The Description page for this app is shown in Figure 12-23.

Figure 12-23: The Description page for Skype.

You may have heard about Skype. It was originally an Internet telephony application that allowed you to make calls from your PC to another PC that also had Skype. Over the years, this application has evolved in terms of technology, the platforms on which it operates, and its future.

At first, Skype was a convenient way to get around traditional telephones. This was particularly economical when calling internationally. (This application traces its roots to a team of developers from Estonia.) The PC was its original platform, but now it happily runs on many smartphone platforms, including Android.

This app has some cool capabilities, like video chat, which I cover in this chapter.

Signing in to Skype

As you can see in Figure 12-23, Skype offers free video chat. However, you still need to sign in to create an account. After you've downloaded and installed Skype, you see the sign-in page for Skype as shown in Figure 12-24. (See Chapter 8 if you need help downloading or installing an application.)

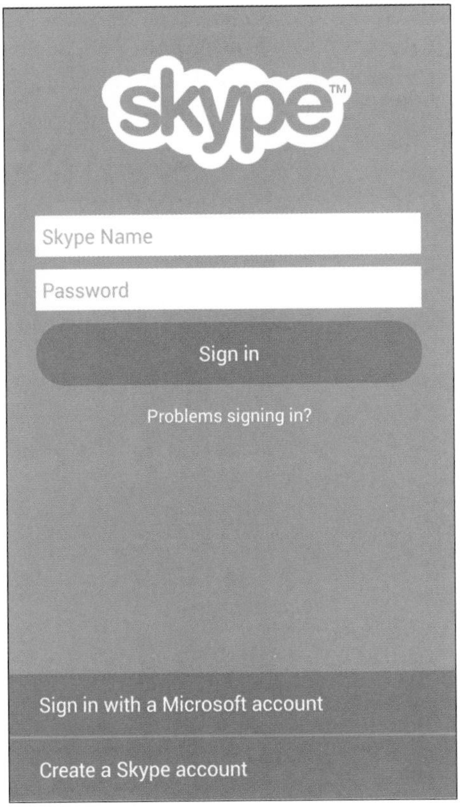

Figure 12-24: The Skype sign-in page.

Here are the three scenarios for getting access to Skype:

- ✔ **Use your existing Skype account:** Do this if you already have a Skype account on, say, your PC.

- ✔ **Sign in with your Microsoft e-mail account:** If you already have an e-mail account with Microsoft, you do not need to create a separate Skype account. If your email address ends in @msn.com, @live.com, or @hotmail.com, you already have a Microsoft e-mail account.

- ✔ **Create a new Skype account:** Use this option if you don't already have a Skype account or Microsoft e-mail account.

If you have a Skype account or a Microsoft account, go ahead and enter them now in the sign-in screen and skip to the next section. If not, tap the Create a Skype Account link at the bottom of the page seen in Figure 12-24.

Before you start entering information, you are greeted with the warning in Figure 12-25.

No need to worry. Your cellular phone is there in case you need to dial 911. Tap I Agree, and you see the Account Creation screen shown in Figure 12-26.

The app is pretty smart. It tries to populate some of the lines on this screen by looking up information from your e-mail and contact database. If you like the options it chooses for you, go ahead and take them. Otherwise, try your own. If the Skype name you enter is available, it's yours. If not, try again.

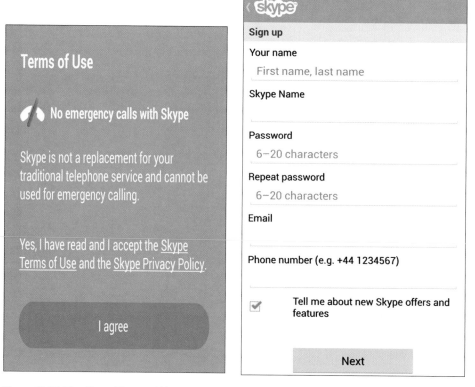

Figure 12-25: The Skype Terms of Use screen.

Figure 12-26: The Skype Account Creation screen.

The Account Creation screen populates the Phone Number field with the ten digits of your telephone number. However, when you try to create an account with this number, it rejects it. It wants the international prefix. That means that you need to enter a +1 before the ten digits we use within the US. Hey, I said the app is pretty smart, not perfect!

Creating Skype contacts

After you create an account, you see the Skype Home screen in Figure 12-27.

Figure 12-27: The Skype Home screen.

The first step in using video chat is to find someone to chat with. This involves finding a contact that also has Skype. When you tap on the Contacts icon in Figure 12-27, it brings up the All Contacts screen shown in Figure 12-28.

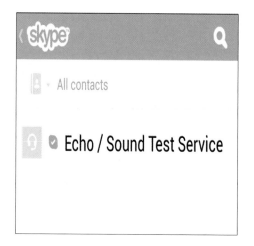

Figure 12-28: The unpopulated Skype All Contacts screen.

To change this situation, tap the Menu button. This brings up three very convenient options:

- **Add Contacts:** You can search Skype's directory for contacts that already have a Skype account.
- **Save Number:** If you know someone with an account, you can manually add their number.
- **Search Address Book:** This is easiest option. Skype takes your Contacts database and compares it to the database of Skype users to find matches.

This takes a while, so you may want to set this up on a charger and let it run overnight. When you come back, your friends will be ready to video chat with you.

When you are done, you have a fully populated All Contacts screen that looks like Figure 12-29.

Setting up a Skype video chat

This is the easy part. If you can dial a phone, you can dial a video chat.

1. **Tap the name of the person with whom you wish to video chat.**

   This brings up a list of connection options shown in Figure 12-30.

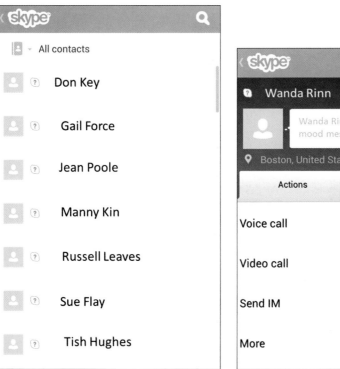

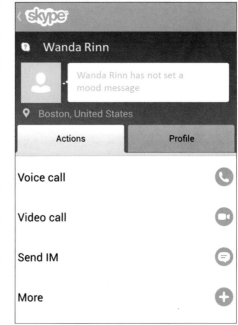

Figure 12-29: The populated Skype All Contacts screen.

Figure 12-30: The Skype dialing screen.

2. **Tap the Video Call option.**

   This brings up the dialing screen, as shown in Figure 12-31.

3. **When your friend answers, you are connected.**

   This brings up a screen like that shown in Figure 12-32.

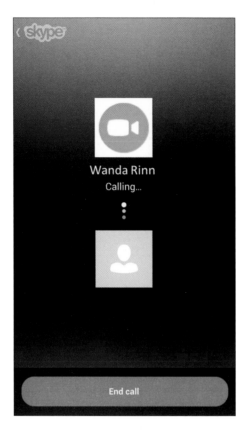

Figure 12-31: The Skype video call dialing screen.

Figure 12-32: A Skype video call.

Part V
Productivity Applications

How do I get to the McDonald's in Kirkland

I will navigate you to mcdonald's in kirkland

When was the war of 1812

June 18, 1812 to December 24, 1814

More

Press the button
or say 'Hi Galaxy'

Visit www.dummies.com/extras/samsunggalaxys4 for info on how to add a security app to your phone.

In this part . . .

- ✔ Downloading your calendars to your phone and uploading new events to your electronic calendar
- ✔ Using mobile Office applications from your phone or from the cloud
- ✔ Dictating an e-mail or text and speaking to Facebook
- ✔ Telling your phone to make a call

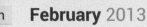
13

Using the Calendar

In This Chapter

▶ Setting up events

▶ Downloading your calendars to your phone

▶ Uploading events to your PC

You might fall in love with your Galaxy S 4 phone so much that you want to ask it out on a date. And speaking of dates, the subject of this chapter is the calendar on your phone. The Galaxy S 4 phone Calendar functions are cool and powerful, and they can make your life easier. And with just a few taps, you can bring all your electronic calendars together to keep your life synchronized.

In this chapter, I show you how to set up the calendar that comes with your phone, which might be all you need. The odds are, though, that you have calendars elsewhere, such as on your work computer. So, I also show you how to integrate all your calendars with your Galaxy S 4 phone. After you read this chapter, you'll have no excuse for missing a meeting.

Some calendars use the term *appointments* for *events*. They are the same idea. I use the term *events*.

Syncing Calendars

Most likely, you already have at least two electronic calendars scattered in different places: a calendar tied to your work computer and a personal calendar. Now, you have a third one to maintain with your Samsung phone that is synced to Gmail.

Bringing together all your electronic calendars to one place, though, is one of the best things about your phone — as long as you're a faithful user of your electronic calendars, that is. To begin this process, you need to provide authorization to the respective places that your calendars are stored. This authorization is necessary to respect your privacy.

If your phone doesn't have a Calendar shortcut on the Home page, seen here, open the Calendar app from your App list. This same app works with the calendar that's stored on your phone and any digital calendars that you add.

When you first open this app, you see a calendar in monthly format, as shown in Figure 13-1. I discuss other calendar views later in this chapter.

Jan	February 2013	Mar		Today		Calendars	+	
Sun	Mon	Tue	Wed	Thu	Fri	Sat		
27	28	29	30	31	1	2		Year
						Groundhog Day		
3	4	5	6	7	8	9		Month
Nick Tesla's Bir	Tom Edison's B		Sig Freud's Bir		Joe Jackson's			
10	11	12	13	14	15	16		Week
		Lincoln's Birth..		Carl Yung's Bir		Albert Einstein		
17	18	19	20	21	22	23		Day
Enrico Fermi's	Gug Marconi's			Franz Boas' Bir		Charles Darwin		
24	25	26	27	28	1	2		List
3	4	5	6	7	8	9		Task
Ilan Punnett Bir..								

Figure 13-1: The monthly calendar display.

When you add an account to your phone, such as your personal or work e-mail account, your Facebook account, or Dropbox, you are asked whether you want to sync your calendar. The default setting is typically every hour.

You may already be a winner!

The calendar on your phone might already be populated with events from your work and personal calendars. Don't be concerned — this is good news! If you've already set up your phone to sync with your e-mail and your calendar (see Chapter 5), your calendars are already synchronizing with your phone.

For most of us, this is adequate. If you are lucky enough to have other people regularly sending your meeting invitations, however, you could get out of sync. Follow these steps to manually tell your phone to sync with your calendars and get all your appointments up to the minute:

1. **From any of the calendar display screens, including the one shown in Figure 13-1, tap the Menu button of the Device Function keys.**

   The Menu screen appears, as shown in Figure 13-2.

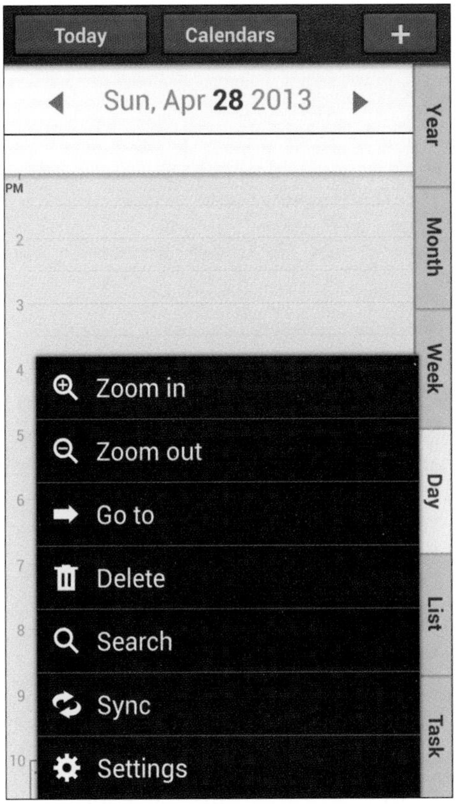

Figure 13-2: The Calendar Menu pop-up.

2. **Tap the Sync button.**

3. **Wait a few moments for the system to sync.**

   All the calendars synced to your phone are listed under the Manage Accounts section. Syncing should not take long, but it does take some time.

Unless you get a warning message that there is a communications problem, your phone now has the latest information on appointments and meeting requests. Your phone continues to automatically sync regardless of how often you ask it to manually sync. It does this in the background, so you may not even notice that changes are going on.

You could encounter scheduling conflicts if others can create events for you on your digital calendar. Be aware of this possibility. It can be annoying or worse when you have a free time slot when talking to someone, offer it to that person, and then find that someone at the office took it. You can avoid this problem by manually syncing your calendar before you tell someone you have a time slot free. I explain how to do this later in this chapter.

Changing Sync Frequency

Every time your phone polls the service, your phone is sending and receiving data, even if there are no changes. It doesn't take much battery to do this, but it does add up. One option to save some battery life is to reduce the sync frequency.

On the other hand, you may find that the lags in updating your calendar are not frequent enough. What if time slots on the calendar on your phone and the calendar at the office keep getting double-booked because of infrequent syncing?

The way to adjust the frequency with which your phone syncs depends on the kind of account that is providing a calendar. The good news is that all of these accounts are stored in one place: the Accounts tab of the Phone settings. When you open this tab, it displays all the e-mail accounts you added in Chapter 5 and some apps that you added in Chapter 8.

To reset the sync frequency, tap on the account, and it presents a hyperlink that allows you to change any sync options that you created.

Setting Calendar Display Preferences

Before you get too far playing around with your calendar, you'll want to choose how you view it.

If you don't have a lot of events on your calendar, using the monthly display shown in Figure 13-1 is probably a fine option. On the other hand, if your day is jam-packed with personal and professional events, the daily or weekly schedules might prove more practical. Switching views is easy. For example, just tap the Week button at the top of the calendar to show the weekly display, as shown in Figure 13-3.

Or, tap the Day button at the top of the calendar to show the daily display, as shown in Figure 13-4.

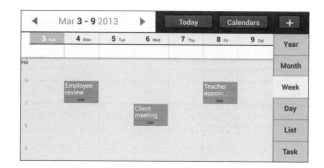

Figure 13-3: The weekly calendar display.

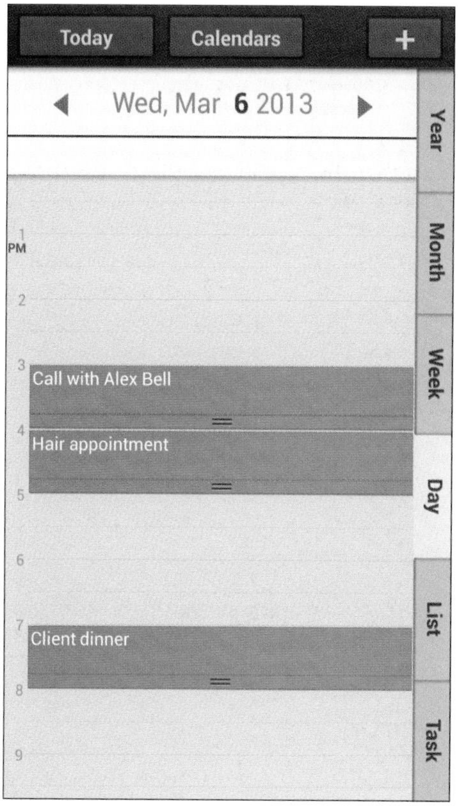

Figure 13-4: The daily calendar display.

To see what upcoming events you have, regardless of the day they're on, you might prefer list view. Tap the List button at the top of the calendar to see a list of your activities, as shown in Figure 13-5.

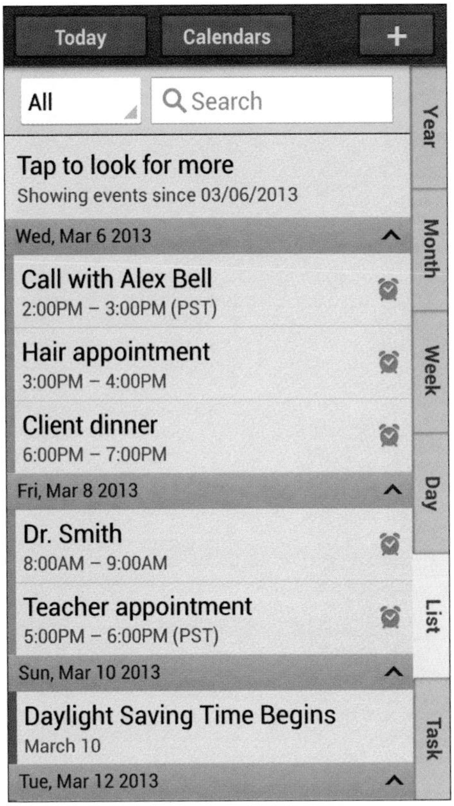

Figure 13-5: The List calendar display.

Setting Other Display Options

In addition to the default display option, you can set other personal preferences, shown in Figure 13-2, for the calendar on your phone. To get to the settings for the calendar, tap the Menu key and tap Settings. This brings up Figure 13-6.

The settings include the following options:

- **View Styles:** If you are not crazy about the way the monthly or weekly calendar appear, try some of the other options that are available.

- **First Day of Week:** The standard in the US is that a week is from Sunday to Saturday. If you prefer the week to start on Saturday or Monday, you can change it here.

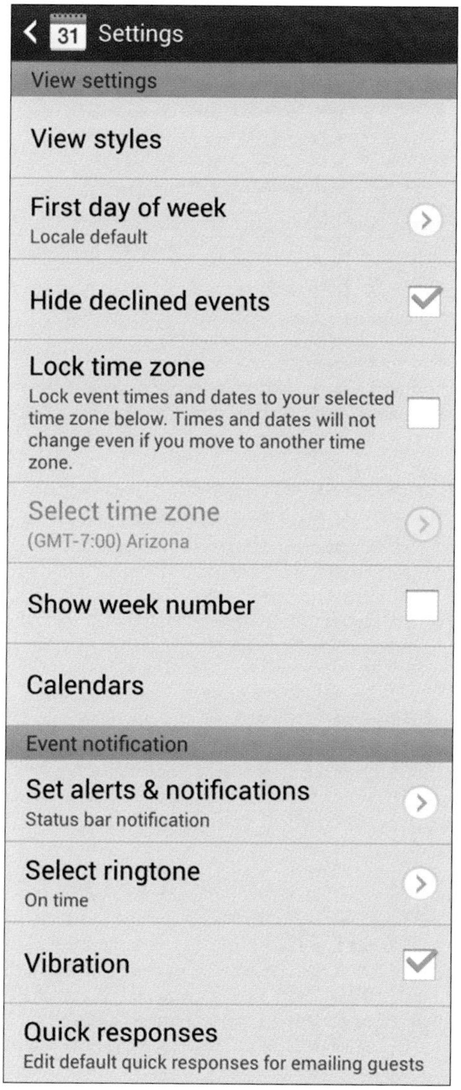

Figure 13-6: The Settings options for the calendar application.

✔ **Hide Declined Events:** For some of us, if we decline an event, we do not care to hear about it again. Others of us may want to keep a reminder of it in case the situation changes or if nothing better comes along. If you want to see events that you have declined, deselect this box.

✔ **Lock Time Zones:** When you travel to a new time zone, your phone will take on the new time zone. Under most circumstances, this is a nice convenience. However, it may be confusing to some. If you prefer that the calendar remain in your home time zone, check this option.

✔ **Select Time Zone:** If you choose to lock in your time zone, here is where you set it. Otherwise, this option is grayed out.

✔ **Show Week Number:** Some people prefer to see the week number on the weekly calendar. If you count yourself among those, check this option.

✔ **Calendars:** This is a listing of the different electronic calendars that are being displayed. You can add another account from here by tapping Add Account at the top of the page. However, you can only change settings on the account, like the sync frequency, for the Accounts tab in the Phone settings.

✔ **Set alerts and Notifications:** When an event is approaching, you can have the phone alert you with a pop-up, signal a notification on the status line, or do nothing. The default is to give you a notification, but you can change that option here.

✔ **Select Ringtone:** If you enable the option to get notifications of events, you can use the Select Ringtone option to play an audio file to announce that its time has arrived.

✔ **Vibration:** Similarly, if you enable the option to get notifications of events, you can have the phone vibrate to announce that it's time for the next event.

✔ **Quick Reponses:** This option is cool. If you get a notification, but something has come up and you can't attend, you can send a message to the meeting organizer. There are some prepared responses you can send or you can create your own.

Creating an Event on the Right Calendar

An important step in using a calendar when mobile is creating an event. It is even more important to make sure that it ends up on the right calendar. This section covers the steps to make this happen.

Creating, editing, and deleting an event

Here's how to create an event on your phone. Start from one of the calendar displays shown in Figures 13-1, 13-3, 13-4, or 13-5. Tap the plus (+) sign. This brings up the pop-up screen shown in Figure 13-7.

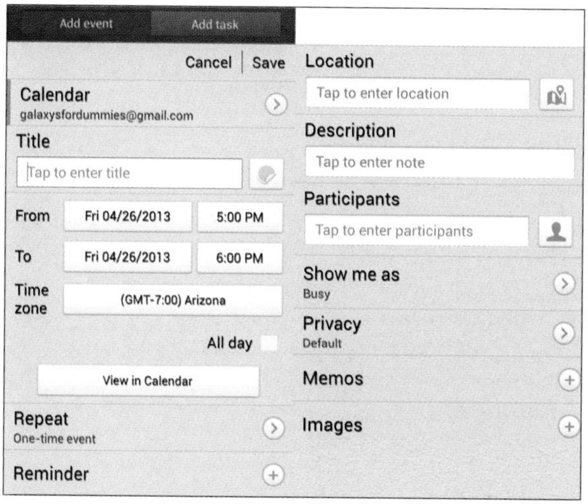

Figure 13-7: The Create Event screen.

The only required information to get things started is a memorable event name and the To and From dates and start/end times.

You need the following information at hand when making an event:

- **Calendar:** Decide on which calendar you want to keep this event. Figure 13-7 shows that this event will be stored on Gmail. When you tap this selection, the phone presents you with the other calendars you have synced to your phone where you can store an event.

- **Title:** Call it something descriptive so you can remember what it is without having to open it up.

- **From and To:** The two entry fields for the date and the start and end times. Select the All Day box if the event is a full-day event.

- **Time Zone:** This field makes it less likely that you will make the common mistake of using the wrong time zone for an appointment.

If you want, you can enter more details on the meeting by adding

- **Repeat:** This option is useful for recurring events, such as weekly meetings.

- **Reminder:** This gives you the option to send out a notification a few minutes or a few hours before the actual event.

- **Location:** 'Nuff said.

- **Description:** This text box is handy for any notes.

- **Participants:** You can invite your contacts to this event. Or not.

✔ **Show Me As:** In some electronic calendars, such as business calendars based upon Microsoft Outlook, you have some privacy options. Some people can see your actual appointments, whereas others can only see if you are free, out of the office, busy, or on vacation. This is where you would set that marker.

✔ **Privacy:** This is the same idea as above, but for non-Outlook based calendars.

✔ **Memos/Images:** Add information that you find useful about that meeting.

After you fill in the obligatory and any optional fields and settings, tap Save. The event is stored in whichever calendar you selected when you sync. If you are worried, go ahead and sync right away.

After you save an event, you can edit or delete it:

✔ **Edit:** Open the event by tapping it from within one of the calendar views. Then, tap the Menu icon. This brings up the option to edit your event. Make your changes and tap Save. It's changed when it syncs.

✔ **Delete:** Open the event by tapping it. Tap the Menu icon. This brings up the option to delete the event. Tap Delete. When a confirmation message appears asking whether you're sure this is what you want to do, tap OK. The event is gone.

You can also create an event by tapping the calendar itself twice. It brings up a pop-up as seen in Figure 13-8. After you name the event, you tap Edit Event Details to get to the screen shown in Figure 13-7.

Add event

5:00PM Friday 04/26/2013

galaxysfordummies@gmail.com

Tap to enter title

Edit event details

Cancel   Save

Figure 13-8: The Create Event pop-up screen.

Keeping events separate and private

When you have multiple calendars stored in one place (in this case, your phone), you might get confused when you want to add a new event. It can be even more confusing when you need to add the real event on one calendar and a placeholder on another.

Say that your boss is a jerk. To retain your sanity, you need to find a new job. You send your resume to the arch-rival firm, Plan B, which has offices across town. Plan B is interested and wants to interview you at 3 p.m. next Tuesday. All good news.

The problem is that your current boss demands that you track your every move on the company calendaring system. His Draconian management style is to berate people if they're not at their desk doing work if they're not at a scheduled meeting. (By the way, I am not making up this scenario.)

You follow my drift. You don't want Snidely Whiplash trudging through your calendar, sniffing out your plans to exit stage left, and making life more miserable if Plan B doesn't work out. Instead, you want to put a reasonable-sounding placeholder on your work calendar, while putting the real event on your personal calendar. You can easily do this from your calendar on your Samsung Galaxy S 4. When you're making the event, you simply tell the phone where you want the event stored, making sure to keep which event belongs where.

The process begins with the Create Event screen shown in Figure 13-7 by tapping the plus (+) sign. The information for the real event is shown in Figure 13-9.

When you save the event, it's stored strictly on your phone and your personal Gmail account. Now you can create a new event, which in this case is a phony doctor's event, on your work calendar. This time, you open an event, as shown in Figure 13-10.

After you save the event, it will be forever more on that calendar until you delete it. Just be sure to keep straight on which calendar you intend to store which event. The name of the calendar on which each event is stored appears under the Calendar heading, as shown in Figures 13-9 and 13-10.

Now, when you look at your calendar on your phone, you see two events at the same time. Check it out in Figure 13-11. The Galaxy S 4 doesn't mind if you make two simultaneous events.

Under the circumstances, this is what you wanted to create. As long as your boss doesn't see your phone, you're safe — to try to find more fulfilling employment, that is.

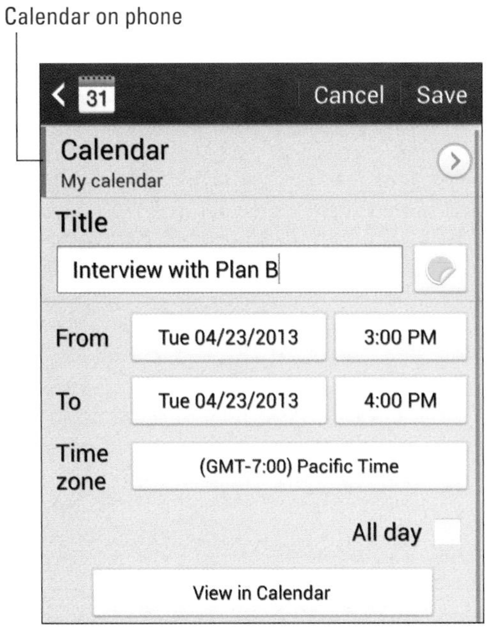

Calendar on phone

Calendar on corporate network

Figure 13-9: The Add an Event screen on your phone.

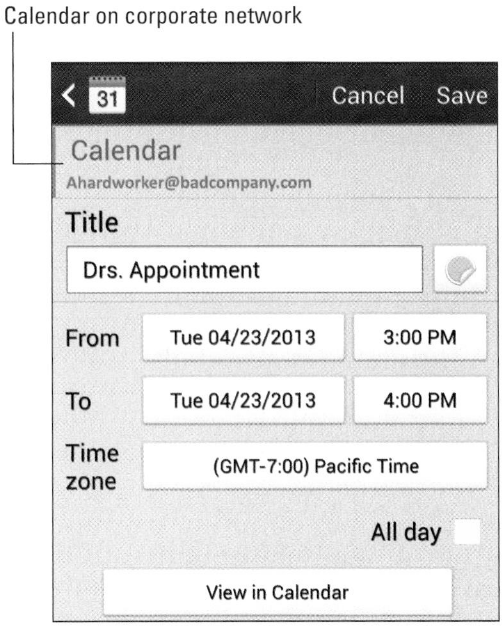

Figure 13-10: The event for your work calendar.

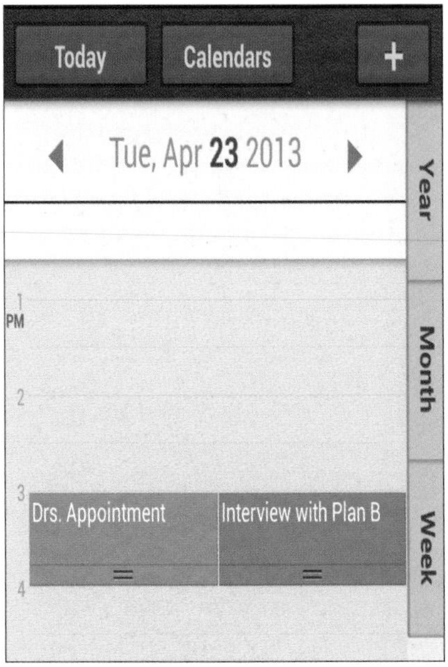

Figure 13-11: Two events on the same day on your phone calendar.

On the Road Again: Taking Your Work with You on Your Phone

In This Chapter

▶ Using Mobile Office applications

▶ Navigating the Office applications in the cloud

▶ Sharing files using your phone

*W*hen you pick up your Galaxy S 4 phone, you are holding as much computing power as was available in a high-end laptop five years ago and a graphics processor that would have made a hard-core gamer envious. So it's not far-fetched to want to work on your Microsoft Office applications, which are relatively modest users of computing power, on your Galaxy S 4 while you are away from your desk. Sure. Why not?

The Galaxy S 4 phone actually doesn't allow you to leave your computer behind for good, for a few reasons. The most basic is that the sizes of the screen and the keyboard aren't conducive for writing novels and other similarly long documents. What makes the most sense is to use your phone to view Office documents and make minor changes, but to leave the hard-core creation and modification efforts to a full-sized PC.

The Polaris Office 5 Suite comes on your phone to let you be productive on the road without the need to pull out your laptop. Depending on what you want to do, you might even be able to leave your heavy laptop at home.

In this chapter, I start with a little introduction on the basics, explore the tools on your phone, and explain how you can use them to your best advantage. Then I walk you through the Polaris Office app so you can know where everything is. Finally, I fill you in on file sharing, so you can get files on and off your phone and out into the world.

Editing Documents

With POLARIS Office 5, you create new documents in .doc and .docx formats or edit your documents with ease.

Editing Sli

With POLARIS Office 5, you can c presentations or edit your pre

POLARIS Office
5_Sample.docx

POLARIS Offic
5_Sample.pptx

Preparing for Using Office Apps

Before I get too far along, I want to explain the capabilities of this solution and the logic behind working with office applications.

Focusing on the Big Three

Microsoft Office applications are the most popular apps for general purpose business productivity. Virtually every business uses Microsoft Office or applications that can interoperate with Microsoft file formats. As you're probably well aware, the heavy hitters are

- **Microsoft Word:** For creating and editing documents. These files use the .doc and .docx suffixes.

- **Microsoft Excel:** For managing spreadsheets, performing numerical analysis, and creating charts. These files end in the .xls and .xlsx suffixes.

- **Microsoft PowerPoint:** For creating and viewing presentations. These files end in the .ppt and .pptx suffixes.

For everything Microsoft Office, check out *Office 2013 For Dummies* or *Office 2010 For Dummies,* by Wallace Wang (John Wiley & Sons, Inc.).

The newest versions of Microsoft Office files are appended with .docx, .xlsx, and .pptx. Polaris can work with the older and newer formats, however. In general, more applications work with the older versions. You don't give up much by using the older version, but you do gain more compatibility with other people who aren't as current. Over time, the discrepancies become less of an issue as more people update to the newer format.

Accessing the Office files

The next challenge in working with Office files is keeping track of the most recent version of whatever file you're working on. The most basic scenario is one in which you're working on a Microsoft Office file yourself. If you have a desktop PC, you're probably accustomed to transferring files among different machines if you want to work on them in different locations, such as home or work. Here are your traditional options:

- **Removable media:** You use a thumb drive or disc to move the file from one PC to another.

- **E-mail:** You e-mail the file from one PC to another.

- **Server:** You save a copy of your file from the first PC on a server that you can access from both the first and second PC.

The first option, unfortunately, is out. Your Galaxy S 4 phone doesn't have a disc drive or a USB port for a thumb drive. You can use the MicroSD cards I explored for transferring music along with the USB holder that I covered in Chapter 12. Frankly, this is enough of a hassle with music files that do not change that much. It is a nightmare for Office files that are changing all the time.

This leaves you with the second two options: using e-mail or using a server. Sending and receiving attachments with text or e-mail that happen to be a Microsoft Office file is probably old hat by now. You receive the e-mail, download the attachment, and work away. When you're done, you save the file to work on later, or you send it back to your PC. I go in to more details later in this chapter.

The server option calls for a little more explanation. By the way, there are two fancy terms for this kind of computing. The first one is *cloud computing*. Readers of a certain age will recall this computing concept as time-sharing, but that name is out of fashion. Cloud computing is in vogue, so this is the terminology I shall use.

There is also an idea called a VPN, or virtual private network. This is fairly common in businesses. Is it similar to cloud computing, but the cloud in this case is the company's computer system.

Cloud computing

The issue of file sharing is integral to getting the most out of the Office applications on your phone. To make it really work, the more Office files you store on the server, the better. It will do you little good if the files you want to see and change are safely stored on your PC, which you dutifully powered off to save energy.

The principle behind this service is that the server appears to your PC and your phone as if it is a drive or memory card that's directly connected. If you know how to copy files from, say, your PC hard drive to a USB thumb drive, you can use a server.

When you tap a file that appears on your phone (comparable to double-clicking a file on your PC), the file is opened, and you can read and edit it. What you might not know is what computer is doing the processing. It could be your phone, and it could also be a computer on the server. Ultimately, you don't really care as long as it works fast and does what you want.

When you're done reading or editing, the file gets saved, secure and accessible, until the next time you want to do something to the file. This is the essence of cloud computing, and your phone can happily participate.

I talked about Dropbox in Chapter 1 and again in Chapter 9. This is a server that you can use for cloud computing. You need to sign up with Dropbox to get access to its server. You need to register, but the good news is that anyone with a Gmail account automatically has a Dropbox account. Just use your e-mail address and password, and you are set. Dropbox gives you multiple GB of storage for your files just for showing up.

And if you don't want to work with Dropbox, you have lots of other choices. These days, many firms offer you access to a server as a backup service at little or no charge.

Using a VPN

The idea behind a VPN is that your phone and the company's data network set up a secret password. They know it is you because you entered your password. Any evil-doers that see your information exchanges would see gibberish. Only your phone and the company computers know how to unscramble the gibberish.

As with checking your business e-mail on your phone, make sure that your company is okay with you accessing files this way. In many cases, it is okay, but some companies have security policies that don't let you have access to every piece of data that the company has ever had while you could be sitting in a competitor's office.

Reading and Editing Files with Your Phone

You can obtain Polaris Office Mobile Viewer from the Play Store for free if it's not already installed on your phone.

Creating a document

To introduce the process, I show you how to create a document on your phone:

1. **On your phone, open the Application list and tap the Polaris Office 5 icon.**

   You need to accept the End User License Agreement. After you do, it displays its Home screen shown in Figure 14-1.

Figure 14-1: The Polaris Home screen on your phone.

2. **Tap the icon for the file type you wish to create, whether it is a Word document, an Excel Spreadsheet, or PowerPoint presentation.**

   The options are

   - *Editing Documents:* Open a blank sheet in Word format (.doc).
   - *Editing Sheets:* Open a blank spreadsheet in Excel spreadsheet format (.xls).
   - *Editing Slides:* Open a blank presentation in PowerPoint format (.ppt).

   This brings up a screen like that shown in Figure 14-2. This is a Word document that describes how to use the app. The details on editing are described in this document.

3. **Tap the Word icon in the upper left corner to save the document.**

   This brings up the options, as shown in Figure 14-3.

Word icon

Figure 14-2: Viewing your Polaris doc on your phone.

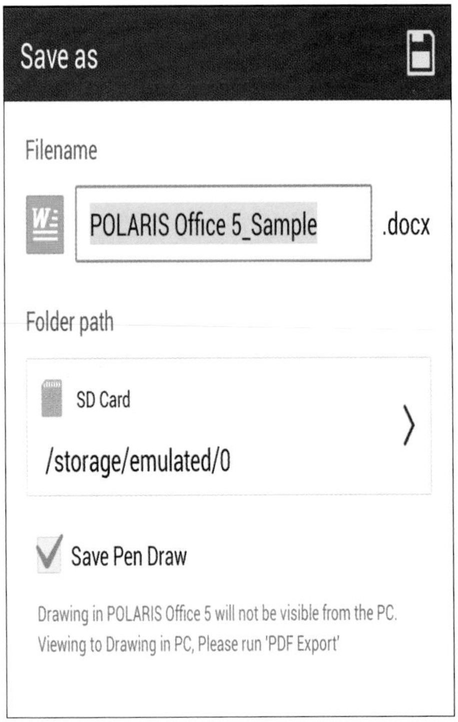

Figure 14-3: The Save As option on the Polaris My Docs page.

In this case, your only option is to save this file in the memory in your phone or on the MicroSD card on your phone if one is installed. More on your other options soon.

4. **To save a document, tap the diskette icon (upper right).**

   The diskette might indeed be a relic of PC technology, but it's still widely used as an icon to mean Save.

   Your phone saves the document on your MicroSD card in the format you selected.

   You follow the same basic process for files in the other formats. If you want to keep this file on your phone forever, you are set. However, read on if you want to do something more with it.

Sending an Office file as an attachment

After a file is saved, it's safe to send it to your home PC or to another PC. When you're ready to e-mail the document to your PC or another PC, do the following:

1. **Tap the Word logo shown in Figure 14-2.**

2. **Tap the Send E-Mail link.**

   You have several choices from the resulting pop-up screen, as shown in Figure 14-4. You can send it as a PDF, but then you cannot edit it any more. Of course, if that is what you want, send it as a PDF by tapping that choice. Otherwise, tap Original.

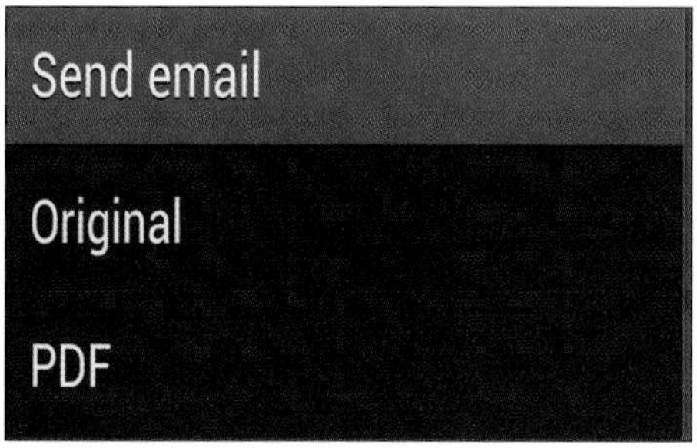

Send email

Original

PDF

Figure 14-4: E-mail file options.

3. **Choose the E-mail option you want to use to send the file.**

4. **Type in the contact or e-mail address.**

   This brings up a blank e-mail screen with your document automatically included as an attachment. This screen is shown in Figure 14-5.

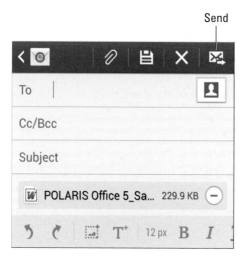

Figure 14-5: The e-mail screen with your doc set as an attachment.

5. **Populate the To text box with an e-mail address (probably from your contact list) and add a subject and a message if you wish.**

6. **Tap Send.**

   The miracle of wireless communication zips the document off to the intended recipient.

If you want the document on your PC, simply address it to yourself.

The process is the same for a Word-, Excel-, and PowerPoint-formatted document.

The formatting of the document on your phone might not be exactly the same as it is when it reappears on your PC. Save yourself time and don't try to format a document on your Galaxy S 4 phone.

Managing Office documents with a server

Regardless of how you send an Office file to or from your phone, the creation and editing steps are the same. Steps 1-4 of the first step list in the preceding section cover the basics. Although you don't have full access to all the editing tools you find for any of the applications, you can do basic editing with the simplified icons at the bottom of the screen.

The next step is to work with files that are stored on a server. As I mention earlier, although you can work with any server. This is easiest to describe, starting from the point of view of the server.

Say that you are writing the great American novel on your PC, but then you want it on your phone to review it and maybe make some minor edits. The first thing you do is move the file to your Dropbox server from your PC. Figure 14-6 is what it looks like on your desktop PC.

Figure 14-6: Dropbox on a PC.

This should look familiar. Here are the steps to view and edit this document on your phone:

1. **Tap the Dropbox icon.**

   This brings up the screen shown in Figure 14-7.

2. **Tap the folder icon on this page with the desired file.**

   In this case, it is the folder that says The Great American Novel as shown in Figure 14-8.

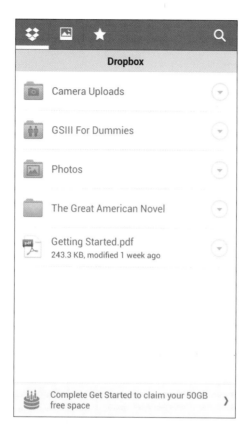

Figure 14-7: Dropbox on the phone.

Figure 14-8: The file in the Dropbox folder.

3. Tap on the file to open it.

The image in Figure 14-9 shows my novel so far.

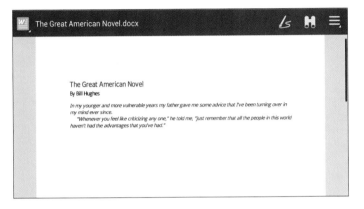

Figure 14-9: The document open in Polaris.

4. Read and/or edit the file as desired.

5. When you're done, tap the Word icon.

This brings up options, including Save.

6. Tap Save.

This saves any changes you have made back to the file stored on Dropbox.

This process works with any Microsoft Office file format. It works with cloud servers other than Dropbox too. It can work the same way with your VPN at the office. The tools are there for you to use.

Chatting Up Your Phone
with S-Voice

In This Chapter

▶ Telling your phone to make a call

▶ Dictating an e-mail or text

▶ Doing a web search without typing

▶ Speaking to Facebook

*E*very science fiction movie worth its salt predicts a world where we speak to computers rather than typing in data. Normal conversation is about 150 words per minute, whereas even an expert typist can only type at 90 WPM. More importantly, talking is the most basic form of communication. The reality is that there are many technical obstacles to having voice recognition match the ideal of a computer perfectly interpreting the meaning of any user's verbal instructions.

That does not stop us from having some fun in the meantime, however! S-Voice, an app that comes with your computer, can handle some basic functions on your phone, including making a phone call, sending an e-mail or a text, searching the Internet, or even updating your Facebook status.

You may love this capability, or you may find it to be a gimmick and not very useful. Either way, you can have some fun with this.

Look Ma! No Hands!

To get started, all you need to do is press the Home button twice. This brings up the screen shown in Figure 15-1.

You can say...

Task
"New task Finish project"

Timer
"Set timer for 1 minute"

Get an answer
"What is the fastest car in the world?"

What would you like to do?

Figure 15-1: The S-Voice Start screen.

Now, ask for what you want. Say you want to call someone.

In the old days, high-end cellular phones would require you to train the voice recognition software to understand the basics of how you speak. No more. Just tell it who you want to call by saying "Call Bill."

Be ready. In just a moment, it calls Bill. It's that easy.

However, if you know several people with the name Bill, it asks in a pleasant female voice which "Bill" you want to call.

A word about intelligent agents

Among computer scientists, S-Voice is called an *intelligent agent*.

S-Voice is a pretty darn good implementation of intelligent agent technology. It's about as good as you can get for doing many of the basic functions of your Galaxy S 4. The list of things you can do with S-Voice includes a pretty long list of the primary capabilities.

But the truth is that this technology is not perfected yet. If you do not want to use an intelligent agent until it is perfected, no one could blame you. Before you dismiss this function as a gimmick, here are a few things to think about:

✔ Normal speech communicates ideas at about 150 words per minute.

✔ A fast typist can type at 40 words per minute.

✔ In handwriting, most people can write 30 words per minute.

You're better off if you can adjust your expectations of asking computers to do things for you by speaking to them. If you use S-Voice for standard commands, it performs remarkably fast and accurately. You can tell your grandkids that you were among the pioneers that used intelligent agents before it was mainstream.

As long as the prediction of an evil intelligent agent HAL in *2001: A Space Odyssey* does not come to pass, this technology will likely become increasingly pervasive as it becomes more reliable.

You may have heard of "Siri" on the iPhone. Siri responds to questions you ask it. The S-Voice app is the same idea, only it responds to the name "Galaxy."

TIP

I refer to the application as S-Voice for the rest of the chapter. Using the name "Galaxy" creates too much confusion between the app and the phone itself.

If you want to call Bill Boyce, a person from your contact list, say "Call Bill Boyce." Within a moment, his phone rings.

A few pointers for using S-Voice. If you hesitate, S-Voice assumes that you are not ready to talk and goes into a sleep mode. To wake it up, just say "Hi Galaxy." It wakes up, ready to resume listening.

I get to the list of things that work with S-Voice soon. For now, try a few of its simple yet valuable capabilities.

Dictating a Text

To send a text, say the words "Send a text." Done.

S-Voice asks you, "Who would you like to message?" Give them the name. It looks up their number from your contact list. It then asks you for your message. Go ahead and say what you would have typed.

S-Voice then converts your words into a message. It displays what it thinks you said in a box similar to Figure 15-2.

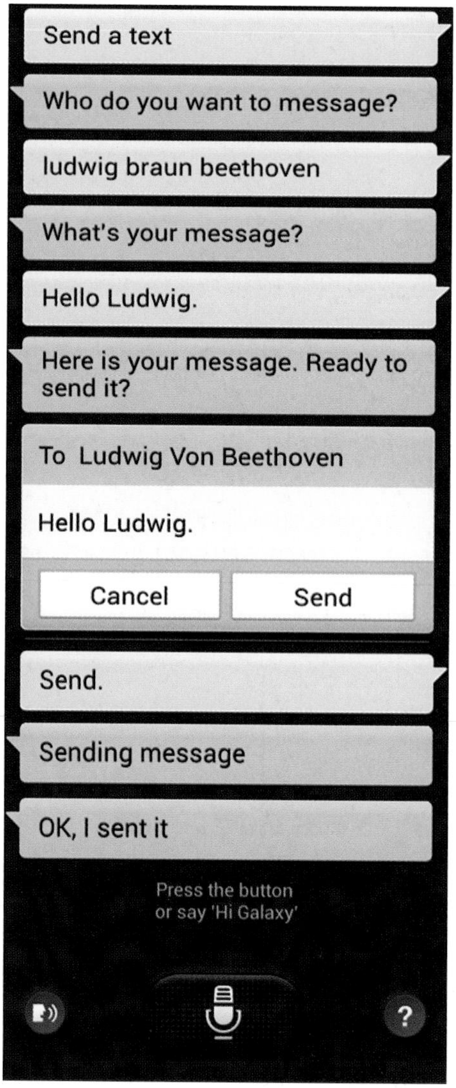

Figure 15-2: The S-Voice texting response box.

Read it before you send it. If it is correct, just say "Send" and off it goes. If it's incorrect, you can say "Cancel," and it won't send that message. You can then try again.

S-Voice is imperfect. For example, you can see in Figure 15-2 that it thought I said "Braun Beethoven" instead of "von Beethoven." It ended up not making a difference in this case.

Preparing to Work with S-Voice

You can ask S-Voice to do all kinds of things on your phone. Some examples include

- Telling you the time
- Setting an alarm
- Turning Wi-Fi on or off
- Telling you the weather forecast
- Setting a count-down timer
- Recording your voice
- Opening an app
- Playing a playlist
- Adding an appointment to your schedule
- Finding a local restaurant, store, or public location
- Navigating to an address or location

All you need to do is ask, and it will do a good job in finding what you want. For example, you can ask for a nearby McDonald's, and S-Voice comes back with some options, as seen in Figure 15-3.

Then, you can ask it to give you direction to the McDonalds that you choose. This causes S-Voice to hand you over to your preferred navigation application. This brings up a screen like the one shown in Figure 15-4.

Now all you need to do is drive there safely and enjoy!

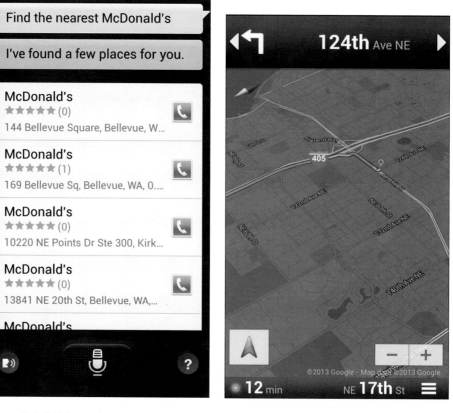

Figure 15-3: S-Voice options on a location.

Figure 15-4: Navigation to the location you requested.

Searching the Web by Voice

These functions so far are pretty darn cool, but they get better. S-Voice has the ability to do some research on your behalf. For example, say that you have a research project, and want to know, "When was the War of 1812?" Ask S-Voice. It comes back with the answer you see in Figure 15-5.

Granted, S-Voice does not see the humor in this question. That is not to say that it does not have a sense of humor. Ask S-Voice, "What is the meaning of life?"

Being familiar with the Douglas Adams series *The Hitchhiker's Guide to the Galaxy* helps you get the joke.

Figure 15-5: S-Voice's response to "When was the war of 1812?"

Updating Your Facebook Status

Of course, nothing really happens in today's world unless it exists on Facebook. S-Voice gives you the tools to update your status without going to the trouble of using your keyboard.

Although you may have already have Facebook on your phone, you still need to introduce S-Voice to your Facebook account. Here's what you do:

1. **From the S-Voice screen, tap the Menu button.**

   This brings up a pop-up menu with the Settings and Driving mode.

2. **Tap Settings.**

   This brings up the options seen in Figure 15-6. Scroll down to the bottom.

3. **Tap on the Log In to Facebook link.**

   If you have not already done so, you need to log into the Facebook app. This brings up the screen in Figure 15-7.

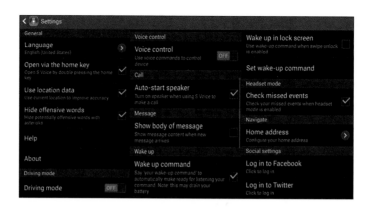

Figure 15-6: The Setting options for S-Voice.

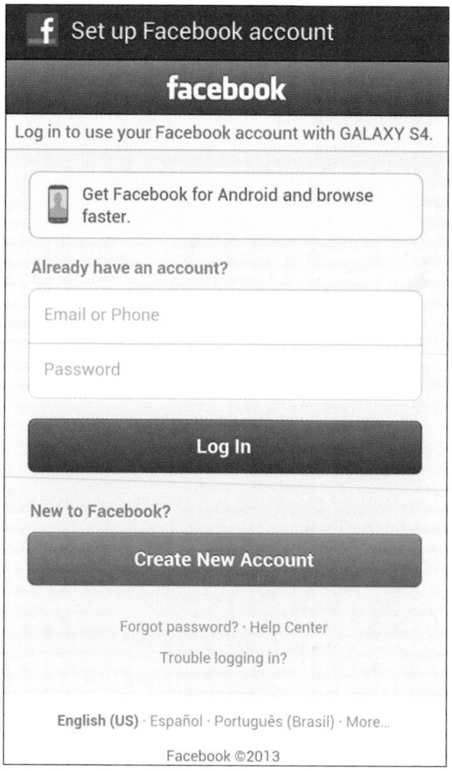

f Set up Facebook account

facebook

Log in to use your Facebook account with GALAXY S4.

Get Facebook for Android and browse faster.

Already have an account?

Email or Phone

Password

Log In

New to Facebook?

Create New Account

Forgot password? · Help Center

Trouble logging in?

English (US) · Español · Português (Brasil) · More...

Facebook ©2013

Figure 15-7: The Facebook login for S-Voice.

4. Enter your Facebook user ID and password.

Ironically, you need to type in this information in the appropriate boxes. S-Voice won't do it for you.

5. Tap Log In.

This installs the app you need on your phone to do this.

6. Tap Allow All.

This gives permission for S-Voice to post on your behalf. (Sheesh. Lawyers.)

Now you are ready to post on your Facebook. To do so, say "Post on Facebook." This brings up the screen in Figure 15-8.

Figure 15-8: A Facebook update on S-Voice.

At this point, it is just like a typical post on Facebook. You share your status and wait for your friends to Like it or comment.

Changing Settings on S-Voice

As shown in Figure 15-6, you can change many settings on S-Voice. Rather than investigate all of them, I look at two.

The first is to change the wake-up command. The default is "Hi, Galaxy." Boring. You can change it to any phrase with four or more syllables.

You may as well have some fun with this. S-Voice is your servant. You can name it anything, such as the name of your former gym teacher, a cheating partner, or the love of your life who got away. You get to tell call it what you want and tell it what to do. There is no one judging you.

Follow the directions in Set Wake-Up Command. It takes you to a new screen and asks you to record your voice saying what you want as your new wake-up command.

Another option you have is on the primary S-Voice screen shown in Figure 15-1. Click the following icon (found at the bottom of the primary S-Voice screen) to turn off the female voice that talks back to you. If you do so, you only see typed responses to you questions and requests.

Some people are annoyed at being talked to by a computer. If you are among that crowd, just let her know that you prefer silence by tapping that icon.

Part VI
The Part of Tens

Visit www.dummies.com/extras/samsunggalaxys4 for a bonus Part of Tens chapter.

In this part . . .

- Getting the most out of your phone
- Protecting yourself if you lose your phone
- Avoiding losing your phone in the first place
- Discovering what features will be coming in future versions

16

Scout Lookout Security Google Wallet Msft office docs Scout Lookout Security Scout Lookout Security Google Wallet Msft office docs Scout Lookout Security Google Wallet M

Ten (Or So) Ways to Make Your Phone Totally Yours

In This Chapter

▶ Getting the most out of your phone

▶ Learning the extra cool features that make this phone so good

▶ Making a personal statement

A cell phone is a very personal device. From the moment you take it out of the box and strip off the packaging, you begin to make it yours. By the end of the first day, even though millions of your type of phone may have been sold, there's no other phone just like yours.

This is the case not only because of the phone calls you make, but because of all the options that you can set on the phone and all the information that you can share over the web. Your contacts, music files, downloaded videos, texts, and favorites make your phone a unique representation of who you are and what's important to you.

Even with all this "you" on your phone, this chapter covers ten-plus ways to further customize your phone beyond what I have already explored. I also explore one way that I suggest that you don't modify your phone!

Your Phone Is Watching You

One of the biggest drains on your battery is the backlight on your screen. Older, dumber smartphones have a preset time when they will automatically shut off. On those phones, you need to push a button to bring the screen back to life.

You, on the other hand, had the foresight and wisdom to buy a Samsung Galaxy S 4 that has Smart Stay. If the front-facing camera recognizes your pretty/handsome face, it keeps the light on.

All you need to enable it is to use your phone. As you use it, the front-facing camera is watching you to learn what you look like.

Making a Statement with Wraps

The Samsung Galaxy S 4 is attractive, but if you want to spruce it up even more, you can get a wrapping (such as from Skinit, www.skinit.com). There are designs to express more of what is important to you. As a side benefit, they can protect your phone from minor scratches.

Figure 16-1 shows some design options for a skin. It comes with cut-outs for speakers, plugs, microphones, and cameras specifically for the Galaxy S 4. Putting the skin on is similar to putting on a decal, although it has a little give in the material to make positioning easier. The skin material and adhesive is super-high-tech and has enough give to allow klutzes like me who struggle with placing regular decals to fit the nooks and crannies of the phone like an expert.

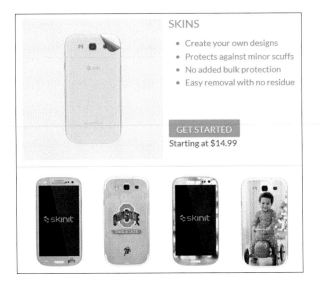

Figure 16-1: Some sample designs.

If you are not crazy about their designs, you can make your own with images of your own choosing. Just be sure that you have the rights to use the images!

Cruising with a Bluetooth Car Speaker

You may have gotten the idea that I am concerned about your safety when you're using your phone. True, but I'm more concerned with *my* safety when you are using your phone. I would like you to have a Bluetooth speaker in your car when driving in my neighborhood, if you please.

Some cars have a built-in Bluetooth speaker that connects to a microphone somewhere on the dash and your car speakers. It is smart enough to sense when there is an incoming call and mutes your music in response.

If you do not have such a setup, there are lots of good options for car speakers. Figure 16-2 shows an example.

Figure 16-2: A Bluetooth car speaker.

Maximizing Shortcuts from Home

You won't spend much time there, but your extended Home screen is critical to your experience with your phone. Ideally, it's where you keep the shortcuts to the places you want to go most frequently with as little clutter as possible. This ideal is probably as likely as keeping your house immaculate day in and day out. Fortunately, keeping your Home screen clutter free is easier than cleaning up in the real world.

To keep Home as tidy and helpful as possible, remember that you can always do the following. Read more about how in Chapter 2.

Add shortcuts to the Home screen for the following things:

- Contacts that bring up the contact so you can then choose to call or text.
- Text addresses that allow you to tap and enter the message you wish to text.
- Directions to a favorite place.
- Folders where you've stored Microsoft Office files.
- Apps or games that you use frequently; see Figure 16-3.

Figure 16-3: A shortcut I've added to the extended Home screen to applications.

You can add shortcuts until the pages of your extended Home screen are full. You can also add more pages to your extended Home screen. You do this by pressing and holding an icon. A silhouette of your extended Home screen pages appears. You add another page by tapping on the silhouette with a plus (+) sign.

You Look Mahvelous: Custom Screen Images

In addition to the shortcuts on your extended Home screen, you can also customize the images that are behind the screen. You can change the background to one of three options:

- Any picture from your Gallery can be virtually stretched across the seven screens of your Home page. (Read more about Gallery in Chapter 9.)

- Choose a neutral background image (similar to the backgrounds on many PCs) from the wallpaper Gallery. Figure 16-4 shows a background image.

Figure 16-4: A wallpaper sample image.

✔ Opt for a "live" wallpaper that responds to touchscreen input.

The pictures from your Gallery and the Wallpaper Gallery are static images. After they're saved to your Home screen, they move only slightly as you scroll across your Home screens.

Personalizing Your App List

The next most important area for enjoying your phone is your Application list. Depending upon your phone, there are two options for personalizing this list:

✔ Switch between list view and grid view.

✔ Change the order of your applications.

Read how to make these changes in Chapter 8.

A Bluetooth-Connected Watch

You are probably familiar with Bluetooth headsets. You may or may not be familiar with Bluetooth-connected watches. Prepare yourself. A few companies make watches that link with your phone.

They do a few things that are neat. First, a watch that connects to your phone automatically switches to the local time zone. This is a nice convenience if you travel.

Next, you can conveniently view texts and other notifications without having to bring out your phone. Unless you wear your phone on your belt, it can be difficult at times to access your phone. If you have one of these watches, you can simply glance at your wrist and get the gist of the message.

Pebble (`http://getpebble.com/`) and i'm Watch (`www.imsmart.com/en`) are two companies shipping products now, but more brands are expected on the market soon.

Tracking Health and Fitness

In addition to the Bluetooth-connected time-pieces, you can use a variety of sensors, or even wear them on your body, to track various metrics. Examples include your heart rate, blood pressure, blood sugar levels, oxygen levels in your bloodstream, and even sleeping patterns.

Each solution is unique, but in general, you have an application on your phone that connects with a sensor. This sensor is often attached to your wrist for the sake of convenience.

This application monitors your status. If you should exceed a pre-set threshold, the application tells your phone what to do. If you are healthy and this sensor is for fitness, your phone can track your progress.

If you need to monitor some health condition, your status may be sent to a caregiver at a suitable priority. For example, if your heart rate is a little elevated, it could send a low-priority message to your doctor. If your condition requires urgent attention, your phone could text a caregiver or specially trained staff member.

You can be assured that you will need to acknowledge a library of disclaimers. At the end of the day, the goal is to increase the chance of getting good information to some who can do something about it.

Fitness buffs can use the Onyx II wireless pulse oximeter from Nonin. An image is seen in Figure 16-5.

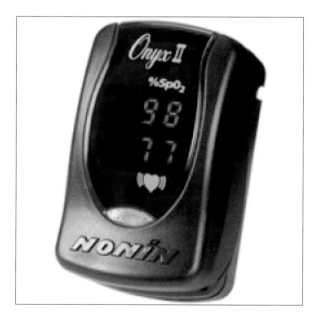

Figure 16-5: A Onyx II wireless pulse oximeter from Nonin.

Diabetics can use the FORA G31 Blood Glucose Monitoring System from TaiDoc Technology Corporation to measure their blood sugar levels, as shown in Figure 16-6.

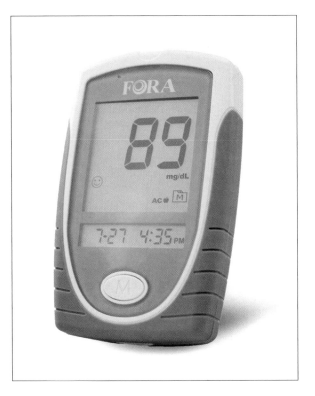

Figure 16-6: The FORA G31 Blood Glucose Monitoring System from TaiDoc.

There are two advantages to you for using these kinds of applications. The first is that you are probably human. As such, you are imperfect. As an imperfect human being, you do not always record your results. Your phone solves this by always recording your results. Plus, your phone probably has better handwriting than you.

In addition, your phone is set up to send the results to a tracking application that is then monitored by a health specialist. They have the knowledge and experience to flag imminent problems or promising trends. This is more sophisticated than what is available from stand-alone monitors.

Buddy Photo-Sharing with Ease

As mentioned earlier, your phone learns what you like. It does not stop there. It can learn what all your friends look like, too.

That wonder of technology you are holding in your hand can identify for you the names of the people in your photo Gallery. It will use images you have used in your Contacts to identify the faces of your friends.

When you take an image if your friend, your phone has the ability to identify, with pretty good accuracy, the name of that friend. It then makes it easy for you to send them a copy of that image. Here is how it goes:

1. **From the Gallery, open the picture.**

2. **Tap the Menu button.**

    The Menu pop-up appears, as shown in Figure 16-7.

3. **Tap the Face Tag option button.**

4. **Tap the Buddy Share option button.**

    The pop-up appears, as shown in Figure 16-8.

    At first, Buddy Share may need some help. If so, tap on the balloon. This brings up your contacts so you select the correct contact manually.

5. **To send this image, tap the E-mail button.**

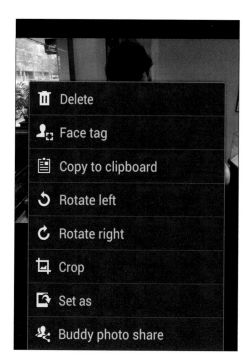

Figure 16-7: The Menu screen from Gallery.

Figure 16-8: A Gallery image with Buddy Share guesses.

It says E-mail, but you can send the message via text too.

As shown in Figure 16-9, you get a pop-up to send it to your buddy's e-mail address or text address (that is, their mobile number).

6. **Tap the Send button, and off it goes!**

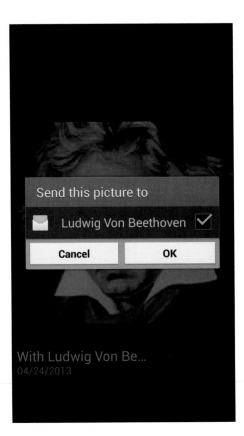

Figure 16-9: The pop-up for Buddy Share.

S Beam Me Up, Scotty

Say you have that image you want to share with your buddy. You can e-mail them the image. You can send them an MMS text message with the image attached. You can set up a Bluetooth connection with them and they can download the image.

Samsung Galaxy S III and S 4 phones offer one more choice. You also have the ability to share information using near field communications or NFC. Simply place the backs of the phones next to each other, and they set up a connection. To set this up, both phones need to turn on this capability. Here is how:

1. **From Settings, tap More Settings.**

2. **Turn on NFC.**

   This option is near the bottom of the screen as shown in Figure 16-10.

Figure 16-10: The More Settings screen.

3. **Turn on the S Beam option.**

   If it's not already on, go ahead and toggle the switch to the On position.

After both phones are on, tap the backs and share what you will.

Driving in Style with a Car Docking Station

Your phone has all those great navigation tools. You can use them in your car by putting your phone on the seat next to you, but that's for amateurs.

Offer your phone a place of honor with a car docking station. It makes it safer to access and easier to use.

Figure 16-11 is the Samsung Vehicle Navigation Mount. This puts your phone where you can see it *and* what is going on around you. It costs about $35, and you can get it at your carrier's store, RadioShack, Best Buy, or online at Amazon.com.

Figure 16-11: A Samsung Vehicle Navigation Mount.

Other brands of vehicle mounts are out there too. Some are made specifically for the Samsung Galaxy S 4. Others are made to fit multiple devices. You may want to get a generic mount if multiple people (with various types of phones) use your car.

Getting a car mount is seen by some as a luxury. Setting your phone on the passenger car seat isn't the worst thing in the world. This may be true if you are a poor college student. My view is that if you have enough of a need to upgrade your navigation software, you have a need for a vehicle mount.

Chapter 17

Ten Ways to Make Your Phone Secure

In This Chapter

▶ Keeping your phone in one piece

▶ Avoiding losing your phone in the first place

▶ Protecting yourself if you do lose your phone

*B*ack in the "old" days, it sure was frustrating to have your regular feature phone lost or stolen. You would lose all your contacts, call history, and texts. Even if you backed up all of your contacts, you would have to re-enter them in your new phone. What a hassle.

The good news is that your smartphone saves all your contacts on your Gmail account. The bad news is that, unless you take some steps that I outline in this chapter, evil-doers could conceivably drain your bank account, get you fired, or even arrested.

Do I have your attention? Think of what would happen if someone were to get access to your PC at home or at work. He or she could wreak havoc on your life.

A malevolent prankster could send an e-mail from your work e-mail address under your name. It could be a rude note to the head of your company. It could also give phony information about an imminent financial collapse of your company to the local newspaper. It could be a threat to the U.S. president, generating a visit from the Secret Service.

Here's the deal: If you have done anything in this book past Chapter 3, I expect that you will want to take steps to protect your smartphone. This is the burden of having a well-connected device. Fortunately, most of the steps are simple and straightforward.

Use a Good Case and Screen Cover

The Samsung Galaxy S 4 is sleek and beautiful. Plus, the front is made of Gorilla Glass from Corning. This stuff is durable and scratch resistant.

So why am I telling you to cover this all up? It's like buying a fancy dress for a prom or wedding and wearing a coat all night. Yup. It is necessary for safe mobile computing.

Speaking from personal experience, dropping a phone on concrete can break some of the innards. The glass may be fine, but the LCD can still crack or the connections become loose. This can happen if you simply keep your phone in a pocket.

There are lots of choices for cases. The most popular are made of silicone, plastic, or leather. There are different styles that meet your needs from many manufacturers. Otterbox is a brand that makes a series of cases made for multiple levels of protection. An example is seen in Figure 17-1.

Figure 17-1: Otterbox cases for the Samsung Galaxy S 4.

You don't just use a good case so you can hand off a clean used phone to the next lucky owner. A case makes it a little less likely that you will lose it.

More significantly, a case protects your phone against damage. If your phone is damaged, you need to mail it or bring it to a repair shop. The problem is that many people who bring their phone in for repair do not wipe the personal information off their device. You really hope that they can pop off the broken piece, pop on a new one, and send you one your way. It is rarely that easy. Typically, you need to leave it in the hands of a stranger for some period of time. For the duration of the repair, those people have access to the information on your phone.

The good news is that most workers who repair phones are professional and will probably delete any information from the phone before they start fixing it.

However, are you sure that you want to trust the professionalism of a stranger? Also, do you really want the hassle of getting a new phone? Probably not, so invest in a good case and screen cover.

Put a Screen Lock on Your Phone

The most basic effort you can take to protect your phone is to put some kind of a screen lock on your phone. If you are connected to a corporate network, they may have a policy on what you must do if you are to access your corporate network. Otherwise, you have eight choices in increasing degrees of security:

- ✔ Unlock with a simple swipe across the screen
- ✔ Unlock with your face
- ✔ Unlock with your face and your voice
- ✔ Unlock with a pattern that you swipe on the screen
- ✔ Unlock with a PIN
- ✔ Unlock with a password
- ✔ Encrypt everything on your phone and unlock with a PIN

The first seven options are selected in the Lock Screen option in Setting. The Encrypt everything on your phone has some serious implications, so I describe it in the "Encrypt Your Device" section of this chapter in more detail.

If you want to choose one of the first seven options, here's what you do:

1. **From the Apps Screen, tap the Settings icon.**

   This should be old hat by now.

2. **Go to the My Device tab.**

3. **Scroll down and tap the Lock Screen option.**

4. **Tap Screen Lock.**

   This brings up the options seen in Figure 17-2.

Each option prompts you through what it needs before establishing your security selection.

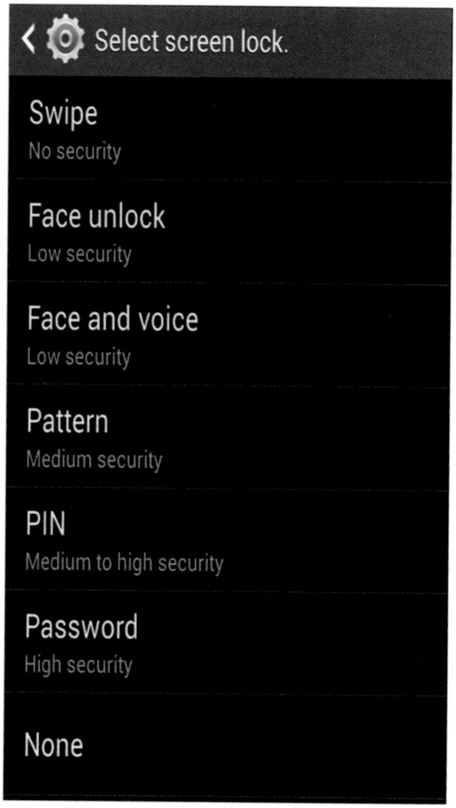

Select screen lock.

Swipe
No security

Face unlock
Low security

Face and voice
Low security

Pattern
Medium security

PIN
Medium to high security

Password
High security

None

Figure 17-2: The Screen Lock options.

For reasons that sort of make sense, your phone uses some terminology that can be confusing. To clarify, the term *Screen Lock* is an option you can select to prevent unauthorized users from getting into your phone. The term *Lock Screen* is short for the action of locking your screen or enabling the Screen Lock option.

Preparing for your Screen Lock option

Regardless of what screen lock you choose, I recommend that you have ready the following choices at hand:

- ✔ A PIN
- ✔ A password

✔ An unlock pattern

✔ A preference on whether you would like to use a PIN or a password

To clarify definitions, a PIN is a series of numbers. In this case, the PIN is four digits. A password is a series of numbers, upper- and lowercase letters, and sometimes special characters, and is typically longer than four characters. A PIN is pretty secure, but a password is usually more secure. Have them both ready, but decide which one you would prefer to use.

The unlock pattern is a design that you draw with your finger on a nine-dot screen as shown in Figure 17-3.

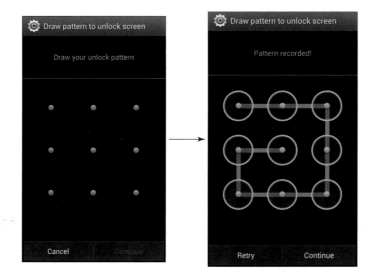

Figure 17-3: The unlock patterns: the blank screen and a sample pattern.

The image on the right in Figure 17-3 shows a sample of a pattern. It happens to include all nine dots. You do not need to use all the dots. The minimum number of dots you must touch is four. The upper limit is nine because you can only touch each dot once. As long as you can remember your pattern, feel free to be creative.

Selecting among the Screen Lock options

The first option, unlocking your phone with a swipe, fools exactly no one and doesn't slow anyone down. Rather than just having the Home screen appear, your phone tells you to swipe your finger on the screen to get to the Home screen. Let's keep going.

The next two options, using facial recognition and using a combination of facial recognition and voice recognition are better, and kind of cool. Your phone has pretty good facial recognition, and most of us bring our faces and voices wherever we go.

That said, these options have some drawbacks. These options don't work 100 percent perfectly. The face recognition is imperfect. In addition, your voice can sound different when you are under stress. Finally, it is not always convenient to use voice recognition, like in a meeting or during a movie.

Although these options are cool, I recommend drawing out a pattern as the minimum screen lock option. Then tap on the Pattern option. The phone asks you to enter your pattern, and then ask you to enter it again. It then asks you to enter a PIN in case you forget your pattern.

The next two options on the Screen Lock screen, PIN and Password, are the most secure, but only as long as you avoid the obvious choices. If you insist upon using the PIN "0000" or "1111" or the word "password" as your password, don't waste your time. It's standard operating procedure within the den of thieves to try these sequences first. That's because so many people use these obvious choices.

If someday you forget your pattern, your PIN, or your password, the only option is to do a complete reset of your phone back to original factory settings. All your texts and stored files will be lost. Try to avoid this fate and remember your pattern, PIN, or password.

Encrypting is serious business, so I describe it in more detail in the next section.

Encrypt Your Device

This is the seventh option for protecting your device. This is an exceptionally secure option: It scrambles every file on your phone into gibberish, which it rapidly descrambles when you need it. This sounds great; however, there are some important considerations to think about.

First, all this scrambling and descrambling takes processing power away from other things, like running the apps. This is hardly noticeable in most cases because your phone is awash in processing power. However, you never know when it might come back to bite you.

Next, after you encrypt your phone, you can never switch your phone back to non-encrypted. With the Screen Lock options, you can use a PIN for a while, and then switch back to the pattern if you want. Not so with the encryption option. You will never, ever, ever, ever, get it back together.

If you encrypt your phone and then forget your password, your phone is what is called *bricked*. That means that its only use in the future would be in house construction as a brick because you're not going to be able to use it as a smartphone any more.

If you are sure that encryption is for you, here are the steps:

1. **From the Apps Screen, tap the Settings icon.**

   Again, this is old hat by now.

2. **Tap the More tab.**

   This is older hat by now.

3. **Scroll down and tap the Security icon.**

   This brings up the options shown in Figure 17-4.

4. **Tap the Encrypt Device option.**

   This brings up the screen shown in Figure 17-5.

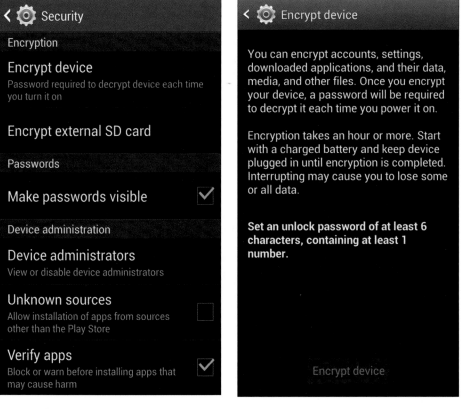

Figure 17-4: The Security settings.

Figure 17-5: The Encryption Warning screen.

As the screen says, have your password ready, the battery at 80 percent or higher, and set aside an hour when you don't need to use your phone. This time, the password must include at least six characters with at least one number. In this case, the password "password1" is also off the table. This is the second password that thieves routinely try.

Put Your Contact Number on the Screensaver

If you have ever found a lost phone, you are faced with a dilemma with multiple choices. Do you

a. Take it to the local lost and found?

b. Take it to a local retail store for their carrier?

c. Try to track down the rightful owner?

d. Ignore it and not get involved?

Kudos if you do a, b, or c. If you chose c, you hope that the owner has not locked the screen. If you did option b, the store hopes that you have not locked the screen. This allows someone to look at phone calls and texts so that they can contact the owner.

If the screen is locked, like I hope yours is, this plan falls apart. . . unless you have cleverly put your contact information on the screen. That makes it easy to contact you.

Do not use your cellular phone number as your contact number. I hope I do not have to explain why.

Here are the steps to put your contact information on your Lock Screen:

1. **From the Apps screen, tap the Settings icon.**

2. **Tap the My Device tab.**

3. **Tap Lock Screen.**

   This brings up the options shown in Figure 17-6.

4. **Tap Lock Screen Widgets.**

   This brings up the options shown in Figure 17-7.

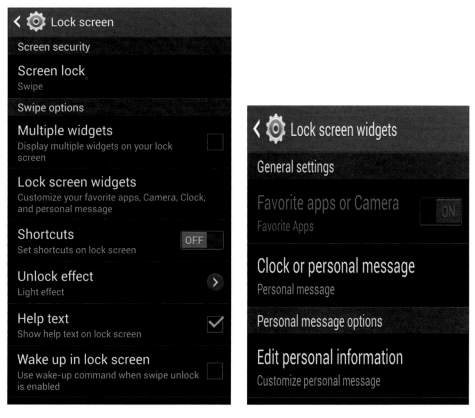

Figure 17-6: The Lock Screen screen.　　　Figure 17-7: The Lock Screen Widgets screen.

5. **Tap Edit Personal Information.**

    This brings up the options shown in Figure 17-8.

    Enter your contact number. This could be a home or work number or an e-mail address, but remember that you don't have much space. After you enter this information, make sure that the Personal Message box on the Lock Screen Widget page is selected and you are set.

If you lose your phone, this makes it easier for whomever finds it to find you. That makes your data safer as fewer people are likely to handle your phone.

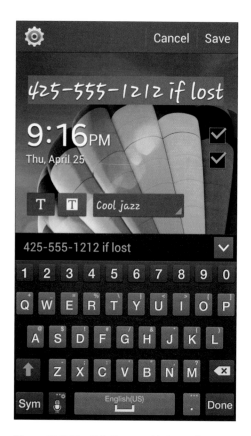

Figure 17-8: The Edit Personal Information screen.

Now before you think that you'll never lose your phone, I should point out some research from the firm In-Stat on this subject. They surveyed a panel of more than 2,000 cellular phone users about how often they had their phone lost or stolen. Interestingly, 99 percent of respondents believed that they were better than average at keeping track of their phone.

It shows that almost all of us think we are pretty good at keeping track of our phone. This same survey found that this panel loses a phone on average every four years. With about 320 million phones in use across the U.S., that means that more than 200,000 phones "sprout legs and walk away" on a daily basis.

Make it easy to get your phone back by making your contact information accessible.

Be Careful with Bluetooth

Some people are concerned that people with a radio scanner can listen in on their voice calls. This was possible, but not easy, in the early days of cellular. Your Galaxy S 4 can only use digital systems, so picking your conversation out of the air is practically impossible.

Some people are concerned that a radio scanner and a computer can pick up your data connection. It is not that simple. Maybe the NSA could get some of your data that way using complicated supercomputing algorithms, but it's much easier for thieves and pranksters to use wired communications to access the accounts of the folks that use "0000" as their PIN and "password" or "password1" as their password.

Perhaps the greatest vulnerability your phone faces is called *bluejacking*, which involves using some simple tricks to gain access to your phone via Bluetooth.

Do a test. The next time you are in a public place, such as a coffee shop, a restaurant, or a train station, turn on Bluetooth. Tap the button that makes you visible to all Bluetooth devices, and then tap Scan. While you are visible, you will see all the other Bluetooth devices that are out there. You will probably find lots of them. If not, try this at an airport. Wow!

If you were trying to pair with another Bluetooth device, you would be prompted to see if you were willing to accept the connection to this device. In this case, you are not.

However, a hacker will see that you are open for pairing, and take this opportunity to use the PIN 0000 to make a connection. When you are actively pairing, you would not accept the offer to pair with an unknown device. If you are visible, the hacker can fool your Bluetooth and force a connection.

After a connection is established, all your information is theirs to use as they will. Here are the steps to protect yourself:

- **Don't pair your phone to another Bluetooth device in a public place.** Believe it or not, crooks go to public places to look for phones in pairing mode. When they pair with a phone, they look for interesting data to steal. It would be nice if these people had more productive hobbies, like Parkour or searching for Bigfoot. However, as long as these folks are out there, it is safer to pair your Bluetooth device in a not-so-public place.

- **Make sure that you know the name of the device with which you want to pair.** You should only pair with that device. Decline if you are not sure or if other Bluetooth devices offer to connect.

✔ **Shorten the default time-out setting.** The default is that you will be visible for two minutes. However, you can go into the menu settings and change the option for Visible Time-out to whatever you want. Make this time shorter than two minutes. Don't set it to Never Time Out. This is like leaving the windows open and the keys in the ignition on your Cadillac Escalade. A shorter time means that you have to be vigilant for less time.

✔ **Check the names of the devices that are paired to your device from time to time.** If you do not recognize the name of a device, click the Settings icon to the right of the unfamiliar name and "unpair" it. Some damage may be done, but hopefully you've nipped it in the bud.

Here's an important point. When handled properly, Bluetooth is as secure as can be. However, a few mistakes can open you up to the human vermin with more technical knowledge than common sense. Don't make those mistakes and you can safely enjoy this capability knowing that all the data on your phone is safe.

Back Up Your Phone

As a responsible user of a PC, I'm sure that you back up your data on a daily basis. That way, if your PC should have a catastrophic failure, you can easily rebuild your system without trouble. (Yeah, right.)

In practice, businesses are pretty good at the discipline of backing up PCs on corporate networks. However, the fact is that most of us are pretty lazy on our personal PCs. Most people back up our PCs only intermittently. I'd be surprised if you ever considered backing up your phone.

You likely have a great deal of valuable information on your phone. Maybe backing up your phone isn't such a bad idea in case it's lost, broken, stolen, or if it has a catastrophic failure. Although much of your information is accessible through your Gmail account, you'll still need to re-build your connections and re-enter your passwords.

Some cellular carriers, like Verizon, offer a backup service preinstalled on your phone: the Backup Assistant. You can access it from Accounts and Sync on your Settings page.

However, have no fear if your phone doesn't come preinstalled with such an application. Many services support Android phones in the Play Store.

Protect Against Malware

One of the main attractions for application developers to write apps for Android is that Google doesn't have an onerous preapproval process for a new app to be placed in the Play Store. This is unlike the Apple App Store or Microsoft Windows Phone Store, where each derivation of an app is validated.

Many developers prefer to avoid bureaucracy. At least in theory, this attracts more developers to do more stuff for Android phones.

However, this approach does expose users like you and me to the potential for malware that can, inadvertently or intentionally, do things that are not advertised. Some of these "things" may be minor annoyances, or they could really mess things up.

Market forces, in the form of negative feedback, are present to kill apps that are badly written or are meant to steal your private data. However, this works only after some poor soul has experienced problems — such as theft of personal information — and reported it.

Rather than simply avoiding new apps, you can download apps to protect the information on your phone. These are available from many of the firms that make antivirus software for your PC. Importantly, many of these antivirus applications are free. If you want a nicer interface and some enhanced features, you can pay a few dollars, but this is not necessary.

Examples include NG Mobile Security and Antivirus, Lookout Security and Antivirus, Kaspersky Mobile Security, and Norton Security Antivirus. If you have inadvertently downloaded an app that includes malicious software, these apps will stop that app.

Don't Download Apps from Just Anywhere

Another way to avoid malware is to use only mobile software distribution sites that are trustworthy. This book has focused exclusively on the Google Play Store. There are a number of other reputable sites where you can download Android apps for your phone, including PocketGear and MobiHand.

Keep in mind that these stores are out looking to withdraw applications that include malicious software. Google uses an internally developed solution they call Bouncer to check for malicious software and remove it from the Play Store. Other mobile software distribution companies have their own approach to addressing this problem. The problem is that policing malicious software is a hit or miss proposition.

As a rule, you should hesitate to download an Android application unless you know where it has been. You are most safe by working with reputable companies. Be very skeptical of any other source of an Android application.

Rescue Your Phone When It Gets Lost

I talked about putting a message on the Lock Screen of your phone. There are also options that allow you to be more proactive than waiting for a Good Samaritan to reach out to your home phone or e-mail.

There are apps that help you find your phone. Here are a few several "lost it" scenarios and some possible solutions for your quandary:

You know that you lost your phone somewhere in your house. You would try calling your own number, but you had your phone set to Vibrate Only mode.

Remote Ring: By sending a text to your phone with the "right" code that you pre-programmed when you set up this service, your phone will ring on its loudest setting, even if you have the ringer set to Vibrate Only.

If you know that your phone is in your house, the accuracy of GPS isn't savvy enough to tell you whether it's lost between the seat cushions of your couch or in the pocket of your raincoat. That's where the Remote Ring feature comes in handy.

You lost your phone while traveling, and have no idea whether you left it in a taxi or at airport security.

Map Current Location: This feature allows you to track, within the accuracy of the GPS signal, the location of your phone. You need access the website of the company with which you arranged to provide this service, and it will show you on a map the rough location of your phone.

If you have a friend that has you as a friend on Latitude, you can call them and get the same information. (Read all about Latitude in Chapter 11.)

Wipe Your Device Clean

As a last ditch option, you can use Mobile Management Software (MMS). MMS software can remotely disable your device or wipe it clean. Here are some of the possible scenarios:

You were robbed, and a thief has your phone.

Remote Lock: This app allows you to create a four-digit pin after your phone has been taken that, when sent to your phone from another cellular phone or a web page, locks down your phone. This is above and beyond the protection you get from your Screen Lock, and prevents further access to applications, phone, and data.

If you know that your phone was stolen — that is, not just lost — do *not* try to track down the thief yourself. Get the police involved and let them know that you have this service on your phone — and that you know where your phone is.

You are a very important executive or international spy. You stored important plans on your phone, and you have reason to believe that the "other side" has stolen your phone to acquire your secrets.

Remote Erase: Also known as Remote Wipe, this option resets the phone to its factory settings, wiping out all the information and settings on your phone.

You can't add Remote Erase *after* you've lost your phone. You must sign up for this kind of service beforehand. It's not possible to remotely download the application to your phone. You need to have your phone in hand when you download and install either a lock or wipe app.

Each of the preceding kinds of applications is available from the Play Store. The simplest security applications are free, but the better quality apps, like the ones mentioned in the antivirus section, are about $10 and require a monthly service fee in the range of up to $5 monthly. Decide what options work for you, consider the price, and protect yourself.

Ten Features to Look for Down the Road

In This Chapter

▷ Controlling home electronics

▷ Finding information and entertainment

▷ Pairing up with Bluetooth devices more easily

*W*ith the power of your Samsung Galaxy S 4 and the flexibility offered in Android applications development, it can be difficult to imagine that even more capabilities could be in the works. In spite of this, the following are ten features that would improve the usability and value of your Galaxy S 4 phone.

Live Status Updates on a Secure Screen

Whether you're using the default wake-up screen or you implemented the Unlock pattern described in Chapter 17, you need to unlock the phone screen to know how many e-mails, texts, voicemails, or updates you have.

The ability to see on the Secure screen how many new e-mails, texts, and voicemails you have waiting would be nice.

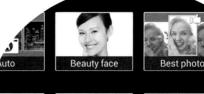

"Galaxy-Ready" as a Marketing Tool

I get it. The iPhone is popular. So everywhere you look, other companies are eager to claim that their products are iPhone-compatible. This includes cars, stereos, speakers, alarm clocks, and all kinds of sundry products.

The best that the Galaxy S product line seems to get is "compatible with some models of Android." Here is the thing. As a whole, Android phones sell about as many devices as iPhones, and the Galaxy S line is the best of these.

These manufacturers of accessories should recognize that there are a great many of us Galaxy S 4 customers and we want you to acknowledge that you can work with us. Maybe then we will consider buying your gizmo or gadget.

Control of Your Home Electronics

Traditional home appliances are getting smarter, offering more capabilities for better performance. A problem they have is that it is complicated to add rows of buttons so that you can control these new capabilities. The next generation of appliances has begun to add a small LCD screen to the appliance. This can look slick, but it costs a lot and is prone to breakage. Also, the fancy capabilities involve pushing a confusing combination of buttons with cryptic messages displayed on a tiny screen.

The latest idea is to omit the screen altogether, and have you control the settings through an application on your phone. Your appliance retains the very basic buttons, but allows you to use the fancy capabilities by setting them through your phone.

For example, your new oven will allow you to turn it on and set the temperature without using a smartphone. However, if you want it to start preheating at 5:30 so you can put in the casserole when you walk in the door, you set that up through your phone.

In practice, many of us have such capabilities on our oven. However, if you do not use these capabilities regularly, it is not intuitive, and finding the instruction manual is often too much of a hassle.

An application written on your Galaxy S 4, on the other hand, can be very intuitive. In just a few clicks, the oven temperature will be ready when you walk in the door.

Even cooler is that you do not need to be nearby. You could be at the office when you change your oven's settings. The oven will never know the difference.

Such capabilities will be available on your washing machine, dryer, security system, sprinklers, thermostat, or refrigerator. This will all be coming soon at an appliance store near you!

Entertainment Selector

The traditional view is that we consumers sit at our TV when we want to be entertained and at our PC when we want to do something productive or communicate electronically. These clear distinctions have blurred since it became possible to watch movies and TV on a PC.

Now that you have HD resolution on your phone, it is not unreasonable to use your phone to essentially do some channel surfing. When you find what you want, and if it's convenient, you switch to the big-screen TV.

Although such a scenario has been technologically possible in the past, the extreme resolution of your phone makes it convenient and a viable alternative to firing up the big-screen TV in another part of the house.

The technology is present to make this vision a reality. However, it is not nearly as convenient as it could be. Today, you need to open the right applications or select the right channels. It would be convenient if your phone could communicate with the TV and have the TV find the right program, and vice versa. It would be slick if the phone could watch your eyes and detect when you have taken them off the TV screen, just like it can when you take your eyes off the phone screen.

Information Finder

Your smartphone, which is turned on all the time, is very handy if you just need to know the location of the 1994 Winter Olympic Games or the title of Virginia Madsen's first movie. (By the way, it's Lillehammer, Norway and the 1983 movie *Class*.)

On the other hand, if you want to write a research report on the relative merits of a flat tax compared to a value-added tax, you are best working on a PC. This latter project is best done with a full keyboard and large screen. The time to turn on the PC, watch it boot up, sign in, and connect with the Internet is small when compared to the time doing the research and writing.

In between these extremes, your phone is increasingly becoming the preferred tool to access information. The ergonomics of the screen, the convenience of the search tools, and the availability of applications all contribute to your phone being the primary source of daily information in lieu of your PC.

What this means to you is that your investment in your next PC should consider how you are using your smartphone. It is possible that you will need less PC, depending upon your information-collection habits.

More and Better Health Sensors

Back in Chapter 16, I mentioned the health and fitness sensors that are starting to come on the market. These are just the beginning.

Currently, you can get devices that track a single function, such as heartbeat or the oxygen level in your blood. There are prototypes of multifunction devices that track several vital signs.

Another factor that is helping drive this market is that the number of smartphone users has been growing like gangbusters over the past few years. The number of smartphones sold exceeded the number of dumb phones as of 2012 and shows no sign of slowing. Phones without health sensors are now the exception rather than the rule.

Finally, these devices have the potential to improve your health. It won't be too long before first responders can have the information to render better services faster because they will know many vital signs before they leave the station.

Better 911 Services

The 911 system has been keeping the U.S. safe for more than 45 years. The dirty secret with this service is that the underlying technology they use to communicate information on where the caller is located has not been updated in a long time.

To put this in perspective, your phone is designed to work with data at up to 300 million bits per second. When you call 911, the phone they use to answer your call is designed to work with data at up to 120 bits per second. (Seriously. I am not making this up.)

Many states and regions are trying to address this problem. This effort is called next-generation 911 or NG911. NG911 promises the ability to take the information you already have on your phone and make it available to the people who are sending you help.

For example, most 911 dispatchers do not have the ability to access the data from the health sensors described in the previous section. With NG911, you can set it up so that the first responders receive your vital signs and EKG when they get the call to respond to your emergency.

With a larger data pipeline between your smartphone and the first responders, you can send anything that is relevant, including medical history, your emergency contacts, insurance data, and whether you have any protection orders against stalkers. All of these help you, regardless of where you happen to be, and your phone is typically there with you.

Simpler Bluetooth Pairing

Paring with Bluetooth devices is pretty darn simple. It would be nice if it were even simpler.

One way is to have the application handle all the settings. Downloading an app is easy from Google Play Store. I would like to see all Bluetooth devices come with an app, even if all the app does is handle the pairing.

More Body English/Less Tapping

Tapping your screen is not hard, but tilting or twisting your screen can be a more natural motion. For example, Nintendo shook up the gaming world back in 2006 when it launched the Wii gaming console with the Wii remote. The Wii remote added an accelerometer, which opened up a new gaming experience by letting the game player communicate with the game through motion.

Well, guess what. Your Samsung Galaxy S 4 has a very accurate accelerometer that can also tell the game what to do with the bowling ball, tennis racket, or whatever.

Up to now, very few applications or games have taken advantage of this capability. All the elements are there in the device to add the ability to interpret gestures. The apps just need to take advantage of this.

Sturdier and Stronger

I have talked about how important it is to have a case to protect your phone. At the end of the day, it would be nice to not need one. I am a big fan of how the phone looks, but the reality is that a responsible owner needs to cover it up with all kinds of silicone and plastic.

Why not offer a least one model that is ruggedized? Indeed, it won't look as sexy as the other models, but it will serve the needs of users that live in the real rough and tumble world.

Index

About the Author

Bill Hughes is an experienced marketing strategy executive with more than two decades of experience in sales, strategic marketing, and business development roles at several leading corporations, including Xerox, Microsoft, IBM, General Electric, Motorola, and U S West Cellular.

Bill has worked with Microsoft to enhance its marketing to mobile applications developers. He also has led initiatives to develop new products and solutions with several high-tech organizations, including Sprint Nextel, Motorola, SBC, and Tyco Electronics.

Bill has been a professor of marketing at the Kellogg School of Management at Northwestern University, where he taught business marketing to graduate MBA students.

Bill also has written articles on this subject for several wireless industry trade magazines. He also has contributed to articles in *USA Today* and *Forbes*. These articles were based upon his research reports written for In-Stat, where he was a principal analyst covering the wireless industry. He specialized in smartphones and the business applications of wireless devices.

Bill graduated with honors with an MBA from the Kellogg School of Management at Northwestern University and earned a Bachelor of Science degree with distinction from the College of Engineering at Cornell University, where he was elected to the Tau Beta Pi Engineering Honorary.

Dedication

I would like to dedicate this book to my late father-in-law, Ronald L. Allen.

Author's Acknowledgments

I need to thank a number of people who helped make this book a reality. First, I would thank my literary agent, Carole Jelen McClendon, of Waterside Publishing, for her support, encouragement, knowledge, and negotiating skills.

I would also like to thank the team at Wiley Publishing: Katie Mohr and Linda Morris. Your expertise helped me through the creative process. Thanks for your guidance.

I would like to thank Thomas Chun and Josh Mason of Samsung Telecommunications America for their assistance.

I would like to acknowledge my sons, Ellis, Arlen, and Quinlan, for being relatively quiet (other than throwing the ball for Indy) while I wrote this book.

Finally, I need to acknowledge the support of my wife, Susan, for her patience during the process that she thought would never end.

Publisher's Acknowledgments

We're proud of this book; please send us your comments at http://dummies.custhelp.com. For other comments, please contact our Customer Care Department within the U.S. at 877-762-2974, outside the U.S. at 317-572-3993, or fax 317-572-4002.

Some of the people who helped bring this book to market include the following:

Acquisitions and Editorial

Senior Acquisitions Editor: Katie Mohr

Project Editor: Linda Morris

Copy Editor: Linda Morris

Technical Editor: Josh Mason

Editorial Assistant: Annie Sullivan

Sr. Editorial Assistant: Cherie Case

Cover Image: © iStockphoto.com / spooh

Composition Services

Project Coordinator: Sheree Montgomery

Layout and Graphics: Carrie A. Cesavice, Jennifer Creasey, Joyce Haughey

Proofreaders: Lindsay Amones, Melissa Cossell, Susan Moritz, Dwight Ramsey

Indexer: BIM Indexing & Proofreading Services

Publishing and Editorial for Technology Dummies

Richard Swadley, Vice President and Executive Group Publisher

Andy Cummings, Vice President and Publisher

Mary Bednarek, Executive Acquisitions Director

Mary C. Corder, Editorial Director

Publishing for Consumer Dummies

Kathleen Nebenhaus, Vice President and Executive Publisher

Composition Services

Debbie Stailey, Director of Composition Services

Math & Science

Algebra I For Dummies,
2nd Edition
978-0-470-55964-2

Anatomy and Physiology
For Dummies,
2nd Edition
978-0-470-92326-9

Astronomy For Dummies,
3rd Edition
978-1-118-37697-3

Biology For Dummies,
2nd Edition
978-0-470-59875-7

Chemistry For Dummies,
2nd Edition
978-1-1180-0730-3

Pre-Algebra Essentials
For Dummies
978-0-470-61838-7

Microsoft Office

Excel 2013 For Dummies
978-1-118-51012-4

Office 2013 All-in-One
For Dummies
978-1-118-51636-2

PowerPoint 2013
For Dummies
978-1-118-50253-2

Word 2013 For Dummies
978-1-118-49123-2

Music

Blues Harmonica
For Dummies
978-1-118-25269-7

Guitar For Dummies,
3rd Edition
978-1-118-11554-1

iPod & iTunes
For Dummies,
10th Edition
978-1-118-50864-0

Programming

Android Application
Development For
Dummies, 2nd Edition
978-1-118-38710-8

iOS 6 Application
Development For Dummies
978-1-118-50880-0

Java For Dummies,
5th Edition
978-0-470-37173-2

Religion & Inspiration

The Bible For Dummies
978-0-7645-5296-0

Buddhism For Dummies,
2nd Edition
978-1-118-02379-2

Catholicism For Dummies,
2nd Edition
978-1-118-07778-8

Self-Help & Relationships

Bipolar Disorder
For Dummies,
2nd Edition
978-1-118-33882-7

Meditation For Dummies,
3rd Edition
978-1-118-29144-3

Seniors

Computers For Seniors
For Dummies,
3rd Edition
978-1-118-11553-4

iPad For Seniors
For Dummies,
5th Edition
978-1-118-49708-1

Social Security
For Dummies
978-1-118-20573-0

Smartphones & Tablets

Android Phones
For Dummies
978-1-118-16952-0

Kindle Fire HD
For Dummies
978-1-118-42223-6

NOOK HD For Dummies,
Portable Edition
978-1-118-39498-4

Surface For Dummies
978-1-118-49634-3

Test Prep

ACT For Dummies,
5th Edition
978-1-118-01259-8

ASVAB For Dummies,
3rd Edition
978-0-470-63760-9

GRE For Dummies,
7th Edition
978-0-470-88921-3

Officer Candidate Tests,
For Dummies
978-0-470-59876-4

Physician's Assistant Exa
For Dummies
978-1-118-11556-5

Series 7 Exam
For Dummies
978-0-470-09932-2

Windows 8

Windows 8 For Dummies
978-1-118-13461-0

Windows 8 For Dummies,
Book + DVD Bundle
978-1-118-27167-4

Windows 8 All-in-One
For Dummies
978-1-118-11920-4

Available in print and e-book formats.

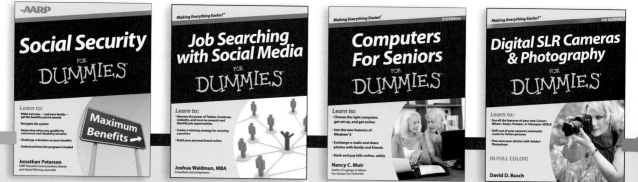

Available wherever books are sold. For more information or to order direct: U.S. customers visit www.Dummies.com or call 1-877-762-297
U.K. customers visit www.Wileyeurope.com or call (0) 1243 843291. Canadian customers visit www.Wiley.ca or call 1-800-567-4797.

Connect with us online at www.facebook.com/fordummies or @fordummies

Take Dummies with you everywhere you go!

Whether you're excited about e-books, want more from the web, must have your mobile apps, or swept up in social media, Dummies makes everything easier .

Dummies products make life easier

- DIY
- Consumer Electronics
- Crafts
- Software
- Cookware
- Hobbies
- Videos
- Music
- Games
- and More!

For more information, go to **Dummies.com®** and search the store by category.

A Wiley Brand